Balkan Struggles

A Century of Civil War, Invasion, Communism and Genocide

Andrew Rawson

Pen & Sword
MILITARY
AN IMPRINT OF PEN & SWORD BOOKS LTD.
YORKSHIRE – PHILADELPHIA

First published in Great Britain in 2020 by
Pen & Sword Military
An imprint of
Pen & Sword Books Ltd
Yorkshire – Philadelphia

ISBN 978 1 52676 144 6

Printed and bound in the UK by TJ Books Ltd, Padstow, Cornwall.

Pen & Sword Books Limited incorporates the imprints of Atlas, Archaeology,
Aviation, Discovery, Family History, Fiction, History, Maritime, Military, Military
Classics, Politics, Select, Transport, True Crime, Air World, Frontline Publishing,
Leo Cooper, Remember When, Seaforth Publishing, The Praetorian Press,
Wharncliffe Local History, Wharncliffe Transport, Wharncliffe True Crime and
White Owl.

For a complete list of Pen & Sword titles please contact

PEN & SWORD BOOKS LIMITED
47 Church Street, Barnsley, South Yorkshire, S70 2AS, England
E-mail: enquiries@pen-and-sword.co.uk
Website: www.pen-and-sword.co.uk

Or
PEN AND SWORD BOOKS
1950 Lawrence Rd, Havertown, PA 19083, USA
E-mail: Uspen-and-sword@casematepublishers.com
Website: www.penandswordbooks.com

Contents

The Balkan states gained control of their territories during the First Balkan War. It may have ended nearly 500 years of rule, but Serbia, Greece, and Montenegro immediately turned on Bulgaria.

Chapter 1

The Balkans Wars

October 1912 to July 1913

The region had been under control of the Ottoman Empire since the 1450s and 1460s, when the armies of Sultan Mehmed II, known as the Conqueror, swept across Serbia and Bosnia. Conflict in the Balkan region may have culminated with two wars in 1912 and 1913, but their origins dated back over thirty years as the people's desire for independence from Ottoman rule increased.

Over 450 years of rule had created an ethnically diverse area, where the rule of three great religions of the world met. Roman Catholicism is still dominant in the north-west, in the state now known as Croatia. Islam is the foremost religion in the south-west region, in the area now shared by Albania and Kosovo. Meanwhile, Orthodox Catholicism is the principal one in the north-east and south-east regions, now known as Serbia, Bulgaria and Greece.

Balkans War Timeline

April 1876	Bulgarian uprising against the Ottoman Empire
June 1876	First Serbian rebellion against the Ottoman Empire
December 1877	Second Serbian uprising against the Ottoman Empire
June 1908	The Young Turk rebellion across the Ottoman Empire
September 1911	Italy goes to war with the Ottoman Empire
May 1912	The Balkan League completed
October 1912	First Balkan War against the Ottoman Empire begins
May 1913	The Treaty of London ends the conflict
June 1913	The Second Balkan War against Bulgaria begins
July 1913	The Bucharest and Constantinople Treaties end the conflict

The Revolts against the Ottoman Empire

Bulgaria rebelled against the Ottoman Empire in April 1876, only for the uprising to be savagely put down. Serbia also declared war in June 1876 but its army was small and poorly equipped, so the Ottomans soon defeated it. A peace was negotiated on the basis that there was a resumption of the status quo but Serbia declared war a second time in December 1877.

The Russian Empire wanted to regain the territories it had lost during the Crimean War and it was also hoping to increase its influence around the Black Sea. So it supported the Balkans, their brother Orthodox States. The Great Eastern Crisis lasted only a few weeks but it ended in defeat for the Ottoman Empire. After 500 years of rule, Bulgaria celebrated its independence under the Treaty of San Stefano. The Congress of Berlin gave Russia and Serbia extra territories but the Austro–Hungarian Empire was given control of Bosnia and Herzegovina. Great Britain was also handed control of Cyprus, giving it a base in the Eastern Mediterranean. Greece then acquired Thessaly in 1881, meaning it had doubled the size of its territories in a short space of time.

The Young Turk Revolution and the Balkan League

Many Turks wanted to modernise their country but the upper and lower classes were looking for different concessions from their government. The Union and Progress Committee were pressing for the constitution to be reinstated, after thirty years of autocratic rule under Abdül Hamid II. Members were known as the Young Turks and they demanded reforms and equality for all subjects across the Ottoman Empire.

The Young Turks were also worried that Macedonia could be lost to either the Russian or Austro–Hungarian Empires. So they encouraged officers who supported their cause to march their troops on Constantinople in June 1908. The government's failure to quell the revolt inspired demonstrations across the Ottoman Empire, forcing Abdül Hamid to reinstate the constitution. However, the Union and Progress Committee failed to win the next election, so members had to try and influence the Empire's politics from the sidelines. Abdül Hamid's attempt to seize power again in April 1909 failed and he was deposed by Sultan Mehmed V.

Events across the Ottoman Empire became increasingly volatile over the next three years. Various laws banned any political parties based on ethnicity, which led to the formation of the Liberal Union. Harsh measures were also introduced to stamp out rebellions across the Balkans, stirring up resentment across the region.

Greece was the first to experience problems over its political difficulties and economic woes. The army had been angry since the debacle of the Greco-Turkish War back in 1897 and a secret officers' group, called the Military League, staged a coup at the Goudi barracks in Athens, in August 1909. It led to the Liberal Party being elected and Prime Minister Eleftherios Venizelos initiating reforms.

Italy went to war with the Ottoman Empire in September 1911, looking to satisfy promises made following the Russo-Turkish War of 1877-8. It seized the North African region called Tripolitania Vilayet (now known as Libya) in North Africa and the Dodecanese islands in the Aegean Sea (off the Anatolian coast).

The Young Turks encouraged Bosnian Muslims to move into the Ottoman Empire where they joined the Albanian Revolt in the spring of 1912. The Albanian Hamidian responded by driving the Young Turks out of Skopje, giving Peter I of Serbia the opportunity to make a treaty with Bulgaria. They then declared Holy War in October 1912, with a view to liberating Albania from the Muslims. Only the Albanians did not see Serbia as their liberator and they launched a coup d'état to unify Eastern Rumelia on its southern border.

In all three cases, the Ottoman Empire was powerless to retake control of the areas, giving the Balkan states the motivation to fight for their own independence. The Balkans region was simmering with both ethnic and religious hatred by the turn of the twentieth century, as Serbia, Greece, Albania and Bulgaria all sought their revenge against the Ottoman Empire. The rise in Balkan nationalism resulted in an alliance between Serbia, Bulgaria, Montenegro and Greece, which was called the Balkan League. Serbia and Bulgaria were the main protagonists and they were both plotting to drive the Ottomans out of south-east Europe and across the Aegean Sea so they could expand their territories. Serbia wanted control of Albania, to give it access to the Adriatic Sea, while Bulgaria wanted Macedonia.

The Young Turks of the Union and Progress Committee used a combination of intimidation and fraud to win the April 1912 election, which became known as the 'Election of Clubs'. Meanwhile, the Balkans' situation was becoming increasingly volatile, as both Macedonia and western Thrace gained their independence. Bulgaria may have had the only large army, while Greece had the only strong navy, but the Ottomans were still demoralised after the conflict with Italy. The Balkan states also knew it would take time to ship troops from Anatolia to the Balkans. So the Balkan League decided to seize the moment and present a united front to drive them out.

The great European powers took different stances during the Balkan conflict, some even supporting different causes to their allies according to their local circumstances. The Austro-Hungarian Empire wanted the Ottoman Empire to continue controlling the Balkans, rather than allowing it to split into small nations. The Germans also supported the Ottoman Empire but it intended to treat the region as a colony. Russia supported the Balkan League because it would counter the threat from the Austro-Hungarian Empire; it also wanted access to the Mediterranean Sea. France refused to support Russia if it went to war with the Austro-Hungarian Empire. Britain supported the Ottomans because it wanted to block Russian intentions in the Eastern Mediterranean. It had also secretly encouraged the Greeks to join the Balkan League for the same reason.

The Austro-Hungarian Empire had the most to consider because it was anxious to stop anyone else increasing their control in the Balkans. However, there were problems. The Slavs were complaining against German-Hungarian control while Serbia was hoping to gain Bosnia. Germany was against a war with the Ottoman Empire, particularly as the Imperial War Council warned that its armies would not be ready until the summer of 1914. But Berlin was anxious for Bulgaria to join the Central Powers, believing it would be able to take over in the Balkans if the Ottoman Empire collapsed.

The First Balkan War

Montenegro was the smallest member of the Balkan League and its declaration of war on 8 October had little effect. But Bulgaria, Serbia and Greece followed suit on 17 October, bringing a combined force of around 750,000 men to bear against the Ottoman Empire. Bulgaria was the most powerful and wanted to advance through eastern Macedonia and Thrace to the Aegean Sea, giving it access to the Mediterranean Sea. Serbia intended to move through western Macedonia to the Aegean, while pinning down Ottoman troops in Epirus on the Adriatic coast.

The Ottomans

By 1912, over half the people living in the European part of the Ottoman Empire were Christians, with the Roman Catholics in the north and the Orthodox Christians in the south. The Empire's army was being reorganised with German help, while several factions struggled to gain control of it. Around 70,000 troops were dismissed in the summer, leaving only 200,000 to man the border. The Western Army faced the Greeks, Serbs and Montenegrins in Macedonia, while the Eastern Army faced the Bulgarians in Thrace. However, the poor rail network would delay redeployment. Reserves had to be shipped across the Aegean Sea.

British naval officers had been employed to train the Ottoman navy, while there were plans to buy new warships from France and Germany. However, the Turkish admirals were reluctant to change their ways and the navy was short of money after the Young Turk revolution. All it could afford was two pre-dreadnought battleships which joined two aging cruisers.

The Bulgarian Theatre

The majority of the Ottoman troops had been deployed facing the Serbs west of Adrianople, leaving only 130,000 in Thrace to fight the 350,000-strong Bulgarian army. Unfortunately, Abdullah Pasha was unaware that Bulgaria and Serbia had made a deal over Macedonia, leaving his troops at a disadvantage.

The Ottoman East Army deployed one corps on the Gallipoli peninsula, to counter rumours of an amphibious assault which never happened. It left too few troops to stop the Bulgarian onslaught against the Edirne-Kırklareli Line in eastern Thrace. Inaccurate information then led to Kirk Kilisse being abandoned, while Adrianople was under siege.

Greek warships had stopped the Ottoman reserves crossing the Aegean Sea, so the Greeks were able to capture Thessaloniki on the Aegean coast. The Bulgarians had also broken through the Lüleburgaz-Karaağaç-Pınarhisar Line. They reached the Sea of Marmara, cutting the Ottoman forces in two only for cholera to ravage the army.

Ottoman reinforcements eventually shored up the Çatalca Line, the final defensive position in front of Constantinople, and they stopped an attack on 17 November 1912. Moscow then told Sofia that Russian troops would attack if Bulgaria captured Constantinople. An armistice was signed on 3 December 1912 but the London peace negotiations were interrupted when the Young Turks deposed Kâmil Pasha's government on 23 January 1913. Fighting resumed with the Ottomans counter-attacking from the Çatalca Line while landing troops on the Gallipoli peninsula. A lull in the fighting followed a Bulgarian withdrawal because neither side wanted to leave their defensive positions.

A prolonged bombardment of Adrianople was followed by the capture of the 50,000 Ottoman garrison on 11 March. However, there was a quarrel over who had taken the city, resulting in a dispute which resulted in the Bulgarians refusing to support Serbian territorial claims. Further arguments over Macedonia resulted in Serbia ending its alliance with Bulgaria because it believed it had fought for nothing.

The Macedonian and Epirus Fronts

The Greeks had deployed a large army in southern Macedonia and they captured Thessaloniki on 9 November, cutting off the Ottomans' Vardar army. However, a smaller Greek army was unable to make any progress in Western Macedonia. The Serbians defeated the Ottomans in northern Macedonia and helped the Bulgarians besiege Edirne in eastern Macedonia.

The Greeks redeployed during the winter months and were able to make progress into Epirus in March 1913. However, Greece then suffered a setback after an anarchist called Alexandros Schinas assassinated King George in Thessaloniki. He was succeeded by his son, Constantine I, the popular commander of the Greek army who was pro-German, changing the Greek stance from pro-Entente to neutral. A final Serbian victory at Monastir drove the Ottomans back into Albania.

Aegean Naval Operations

The Greek fleet secured the Aegean islands when war broke out, so they would be ready to attack any ships sailing out of the Dardanelle Straits. They also secured Preveza on the west coast of Greece, securing the entrance to the Ionian Sea. It meant the Greek ships would be able to stop transports crossing either the Aegean or Ionian Seas, leaving 250,000 Ottoman troops unable to join the war in the Balkans.

The situation led to Admiral Tahir Bey replacing Admiral Ramiz Naman Bey and he immediately tried to draw the Greek fleet into a battle. The two fleets eventually clashed at the entrance to the Dardanelle Straits on 16 December and the Greeks won the battle of Elli. A week later a Greek submarine fired torpedoes for the first time in history.

Captain Ramiz Bey planned to attack the Greek anchorage by sending a fast cruiser to draw a Greek blockade away from Lemnos Island early on 14 January 1913. However, Rear Admiral Pavlos Kountouriotis correctly assumed the single ship was a decoy and his fleet was able to intercept the Ottoman fleet when it left the Dardanelle Straits four days later. The Ottoman Navy retired to Constantinople harbour and never re-entered the Aegean Sea again. It was, however, targeted during the first ever air raid directed against ships on 5 February.

The Ottoman Defeat and Aftermath

The Ottoman government had gone to war before its armies had mobilised because the War Minister, Nazim Pasha, had incorrectly promised that the armed services were ready to fight. The Treaty of London ended the conflict on 30 May 1913 and most of the Ottoman territories west of Constantinople were divided between the Balkan League nations, as were many of the Aegean islands. Serbia and Greece divided Macedonia, while the new nation of Albania was created on the Adriatic coast. However, Bulgaria was unhappy that it had only received part of Thrace, resulting in Serbia and Greece becoming allies to counter the threat. A second treaty may have been signed but the seeds had been sown for another conflict.

The nations had settled their differences but the people were left with their own decisions to make once the new borders had been decided. People were forced to accept their new nationalities and while many were baptised by the Orthodox Church, those who refused to convert headed for the Ottoman Empire. Ethnic and religious violence followed: people were evicted and their villages were burnt to the ground.

The Second Balkan War

The Balkan League had pushed the Ottoman Empire out of south-east Europe but there were arguments over who would rule Macedonia. Serbia and Bulgaria may have secretly agreed to share northern Macedonia but the Serbs had advanced further south than expected, while the Greeks had taken Thessaloniki. The Serbs refused to withdraw from the captured territory because the creation of Albania would leave them with little territory. Both Serbia and Russia ended their alliance with Bulgaria over the argument about Macedonia. So, the Bulgarians decided to seize what they thought was rightly theirs, only to discover that Serbia and Greece had signed an agreement to protect themselves against just that.

On 16 June 1913, Tsar Ferdinand ordered the mobilisation of Bulgaria's armed forces, but Prime Minister Stoyan Danev's government asked General Mihail Savov not to, delaying the invasion of Serbia and Greece. The Tsar replaced him with General Radko Dimitriev, and while there may have been 600,000 troops ready to retake Macedonia, there were only enough rifles to arm half of them.

The Greeks attacked while the Bulgarians procrastinated and they advanced towards Sofia. The Bulgarian offensive eventually started on 26 June, only to be driven back through Dojran by a counter-attack. The Serbs stopped the attack across the River Zletovska on 29 June and drove it back behind the River Bregalnica. One Bulgarian division was even forced to surrender en masse and General Mihail Savov had to personally take command of the front line to stop the Serbs advancing into western Bulgaria.

The Greeks made contact with the Serbs on 11 July and they advanced side-by-side along the River Struma. Amphibious landings by Greek troops then cut off large numbers of Bulgarians from the Aegean Sea. The Serbs stopped advancing when they had taken all the territory they wanted; however, the Greeks continued advancing along the Struma valley. The Bulgarians ambushed them in the Kresna Gorge but they managed to break out and kept heading north, deeper into enemy territory.

Romania declared war on 10 July, leaving the Bulgarians fighting a war on two fronts. Its troops crossed the border and some cut off the north-west corner of the country as they advanced to contact the Serbs. Some Romanian troops were closing in on Sofia when the Ottomans attacked on 29 July, forcing the Bulgaria troops out of Eastern Thrace. Moscow finally decided to intervene and the Russian army prepared to cross the Caucasus Mountains, while its fleet sailed towards Constantinople.

Bulgaria may have felt aggrieved by having to give up so much of Macedonia following the First Balkan War, but attacking Greece and Serbia in the Second Balkan War only made matters worse. Sofia had to announce a truce and ask Russia to arbitrate in the conflict. It then sent representatives to the peace negotiations in the Romanian capital, Bucharest. Neither the Serbs nor the Greeks wanted to talk, but King Carol agreed to stop his Romanian troops from entering Sofia.

Bulgaria signed the Treaty of Bucharest with Serbia, Montenegro, Romania and Greece on 10 August 1913 and was forced to give away large amounts of territory. Serbia extended its border south, to include central Vardar Macedonia. Meanwhile, Bulgaria was given part of Macedonia, Pirin Macedonia and Western Thrace, giving it access to the Aegean Sea. It also had to hand Southern Dobruja, on its north-east border, to Romania. Greece was given parts of Epirus and Macedonia beyond its northern border.

Sofia would later agree the Treaty of Constantinople with Constantinople. The Ottoman Empire took control of Eastern Thrace, giving Constantinople a larger foothold in south-east Europe. It also set up a provisional government to control Western Thrace. The Ottomans would also sign treaties with Greece, Serbia and finally a secret treaty with Bulgaria, after the World War broke out.

Serbia gained parts of northern Macedonia making it the most powerful nation south of the River Danube. It had also gained around one and a half million people and they would face oppression, imprisonment, exile and even death. Serbia may have settled its southern border but it now faced arguments with the Austro-Hungarian Empire over its northern border. The situation would result in a conflict just a few months later; one which quickly escalated into the First World War.

Another outcome of the Second Balkan War was the validation of an independent Albania at the London Conference of July 1913. It took territory from Serbia and Greece, creating resentment in both countries. An uprising in the Greek section resulted in the area being promised autonomy under the Treaty of Corfu, except the outbreak of World War I stopped it being implemented.

The Second Balkan War had ended Russia's chances of getting access to the Mediterranean Sea. It also brought an end to the Balkan League and the Russian buffer zone in the Balkans. Russia's support for Serbia resulted in Belgrade being isolated in its standoff with the mighty Austro-Hungarian Empire. It also ended relations between Moscow and Sofia, which convinced Bulgaria to join the Central Powers. Russia's desire to support its only Balkan ally increased, which led the Austria-Hungarians and the Germans to view Serbia as a Russian satellite state.

Conflict had raged across the Balkans for the second time in twelve months, and the two conflicts had resulted in the deaths of 142,000 soldiers in action; another 82,000 had succumbed to illness or disease. Untold numbers of civilians had also died or been displaced from their homes.

Genocide across Anatolia

Horrific events had been taking place across the Ottoman Empire and although they took place outside the Balkans they had their roots in the Balkan Wars. The aftershock of the religious and ethnic cleansing of Anatolia (the Asian part of the Ottoman Empire, now known as Turkey) would continue both through and after the World War.

Around 2.5 million Christian Armenians lived in Eastern Anatolia. Most were peasants who sometimes experienced ill treatment at the hands of the Muslim Kurds. A few Armenian activists had called for an independent Armenian state but most suffered in silence. Calls for reforms and protests by many failing to pay their taxes in 1894 led to a violent backlash. Tens of thousands of Armenians were killed or died of starvation and disease in what were called the Hamidian massacres. Many more were made homeless, robbed or were forced to convert to Islam. The slaughter might have come to an end in 1897 but Sultan Abdul Hadid increased the restrictions against the Armenians even further.

The takeover of the Ottoman Empire by the Young Turks in 1908 initially raised Armenian hopes for equality and religious tolerance. But they were soon dashed and thousands were killed in riots in 1909. Hatred against the Armenians increased following the First Balkan War because the Ottoman Muslims blamed the loss of European territory on what they saw as traitorous behaviour by the Balkan Christians. The hundreds of thousands of European Muslims pouring into Anatolia also saw them as their enemy. European interference in the Armenian situation only served to increase the Turks' animosity towards their neighbours. The Muslims increasingly sought revenge against the Armenian Christians.

The Turkish national movement wanted all the ethnic Greeks removed from the Ottoman Empire in the wake of the First Balkan War. Forced expulsions from eastern Thrace and the Aegean coast began in spring 1913 and any resistance was brutally put down. The following June, the coastal town of Phocaea (now Foça) was destroyed; those who survived the massacre fled to Greece.

All Greek men were conscripted into Labour Battalions and deployed across Anatolia in the summer 1914. They were used as forced labour in harsh conditions and many would be worked to death. Meanwhile, their families were driven from their villages so that Muslim refugees could take their place.

Ottoman policy was reformed after November 1914 to appease the Germans. The new plan was to remove Greeks from all military zones on the grounds of security, and families were again deported and their villages looted to make way for Muslims. The Turks also wanted the Armenians living along the Russian border to fight for the Ottoman Empire. However, *Dashnaktsutyun* (the main Armenian political party) refused to recruit anyone from Russian territory, in an act of defiance considered a betrayal by the Turks.

The Ottoman defeat at the battle of Sarıkamış in January 1915 was unfairly blamed on the Armenians. Even so, Enver Paşa gave orders for his troops to disband all the Armenian military units before executing their soldiers. Mass killings of Armenian civilians along the Russian border followed and any resistance resulted in further bloodshed. Widespread deportations, under the guise of securing the Russian border, were accompanied by more violence. Those who survived the carnage were marched long distances to remote concentration camps across Syria, where many would die of starvation or disease.

The persecution of Greeks had also continued apace. The Minister of War, Ismail Enver, stated that the Empire's policy was to end the Greek problem in the same way it had 'solved the Armenian problem'; in other words, through massacres and deportations. State policy changed in the autumn of 1916, because the Russians were advancing across Anatolia. Greece was expected to join the Allies and so the brutal policies of conscripting men and deporting women was reinstated. Some Greek men who lived along the Black Sea coast decided to fight with the help of Russian supplies. Others joined the Caucasus Division and fought the Ottomans while helping Greek refugees escape.

Ottoman policies resulted in the ethnic cleansing of Anatolia. Estimates vary but anywhere up to one and a half million Armenians died in what has been acknowledged as the world's first modern genocide, in which deliberate and systematic killings were carried out. By the time the Turks had finished, around ninety per cent of the Armenians were either dead or had been deported; the few survivors had been forced to convert to Islam. Around half a million Greeks had also been deported while estimates for the death toll range from 300,000 to 750,000, and all the churches and buildings relating to the Eastern Orthodox Church across Anatolia were destroyed.

Problems between the Austro–Hungarian Empire and Serbia led to the spark which started the Great War. Germany, Bulgaria, Italy, Romania and Greece would all be drawn into the inconclusive conflict across the Balkans.

Chapter 2

The Great War

August 1914 to November 1918

The Balkans may have just emerged from the second of two conflicts in just two years but it was still volatile because the Germans, Austro-Hungarians and Bulgarians were in a stand-off with the Russians. The area was a powder keg which only needed a spark to set the Entente and the Central Powers against each other. That spark occurred on 28 June 1914, when members of the Young Bosnia movement set out to kill the heir to the Austro-Hungarian throne in Sarajevo. It was their way of seeking independence for the southern Slavic provinces from the huge Empire.

What follows is a study of each nation's experience during the Great War.

The Great War Timeline

28 June 1914	The assassination of Archduke Franz Ferdinand of Austria
28 July 1914	The Austro-Hungarian Empire and Serbia are at war
April 1915	The Allies invade Gallipoli
September 1915	Bulgaria joins the Central Powers
October 1915	The Allies advance north from Thessaloniki
October 1915	German and Austro-Hungarian Empires attack Serbia, followed by Bulgaria
January 1916	The Austro-Hungarian Empire attacks the Montenegrin army
February 1916	The Serbs are evacuated from the mainland
August 1916	The Germans attack the Allies around Thessaloniki
June 1917	Greece declares war against the Central Powers
May 1918	The Greeks defeat the Bulgarians and they do not react

September 1918	French and Serbian troops break though the Bulgarian lines
29 September 1918	Bulgaria surrenders
26 October	The Ottoman Empire signs the Armistice of Mudros
3 November	The Austro-Hungarian Empire signs an armistice
11 November	A general armistice comes into effect across Europe

Serbia during the Great War

The first attempt to kill the heir to the Austro-Hungarian throne in Sarajevo on 28 June 1914 failed. But Gavrilo Princip managed to assassinate Archduke Franz Ferdinand, and his wife Sophie, Duchess of Hohenberg, at the second attempt. The Austro-Hungarian Empire issued an ultimatum which Serbia did not comply with, because it was looking for an excuse to invade. Serbia agreed to eight of the ten demands but the two countries still entered a state of war on 28 July 1914. Russia declared its support for Serbia, triggering an escalation of the conflict which drew in Germany, France and Great Britain over the week that followed.

There were violent anti-Serb demonstrations and little quarter was given as the Bulgarian and Austro-Hungarian armies advanced across Serb territory, systematically executing soldiers, murdering civilians and burning villages. Serbia may have had an experienced army but it was worn out after the recent Balkan Wars. Even so, the small army would hold its own until the Russians defeated the Austro-Hungarians.

The Austro-Hungarian Empire may have only had a modest standing army of 450,000 men, but it had soon increased to two million with another 1,350,000 in reserve to replace casualties. The original plan was for three armies to attack Serbia but many troops had to be transferred to Galicia to counter the Russian intervention. It left only 285,000 men to attack Serbia and some of them identified with the Serb cause. The multi-national status of the Empire meant that the soldiers often spoke different languages to their comrades and their officers. It meant that their training had been basic, and orders had to be communicated by signals.

The Serbian army was much smaller and was organised into three bans, or *poziv*, according to age. The first ban served in the front line, the second were used as replacements and the third worked on the lines of communication. The soldiers were organised into four armies but few units were equipped with modern weapons or equipment, and all were short of ammunition. Russia had promised to make up the deficit but it would take time to deliver the supplies.

The Austro-Hungarian artillery started shelling Belgrade on 29 July 1914, while the infantry prepared to cross the River Drina on 12 August. General Liborius von Frank was looking to win a victory in northern Bosnia, in time to announce it on Emperor Franz Joseph's birthday. However, the Serbs reinforced the area and the Austro-Hungarians were driven back rather than celebrating, in what became known as the battle of Cer.

The Serbs countered by advancing across the Sava river, to interfere with the transfer of troops from Syrmia to the Russian front. They were soon driven back, after suffering many casualties, but General Petar Bojović decided to try again in September. This time their offensive north-east of Sarajevo ended in stalemate due to a lack of ammunition.

The Austro-Hungarians renewed their offensive on 5 November and they pushed the Serbs back across the Kolubara River and out of Belgrade. A lack of ammunition was again the problem until fresh supplies allowed the Serbs to recapture their capital on 15 December. The year ended with stalemate in the trenches after a combined casualty count of over 280,000 in just five months. Hunger and disease took the place of combat casualties over the winter months, as hundreds of thousands of Serbs died of typhus.

The Serb Parliament declared they wanted to unify all the Serbs, Croatians and Slovenians when it made the Niš Declaration. Meanwhile, the Germans were urging the Austro-Hungarians to defeat Serbia, because they wanted a rail link to connect with their ally, the Ottomans. Both sides still wanted Bulgaria as an ally but the Central Powers bribed Sofia with an offer of Serbian territory. King Ferdinand accepted and signed a treaty with Germany, which forced the Allies to send divisions to Greece. They were en route as the German and Austro-Hungarian armies advanced across the River Danube and entered Belgrade.

The Bulgarian armies had joined in the offensive on 14 October and they were soon driving the Serbs back towards Niš and Skopje. Field Marshal Radomira Putnik was desperate for his men to escape from Kosovo but the only way to escape was through the Albanian mountains. Thousands of civilians joined the Serbian retreat, fearful of the bloodthirsty Austro-Hungarians.

Only 100,000 Serbs (soldiers and civilians) survived the long, desperate march to the Adriatic coast where they found Allied ships waiting to evacuate them. Around 90,000 of their comrades and families had succumbed to the severe weather conditions, while another 175,000 had been taken prisoner. The evacuation to Corfu was complete by February 1916 and everyone would be later shipped to mainland Greece.

The Allies eventually commenced their advance north from Thessaloniki in October 1915. General Maurice Sarrail wanted to advance up the Vardar River but the British commander refused, leaving the French troops to go on alone. They were soon defeated at Krivolak and then the British were driven back during the battle of Kosturino. It meant that all of Sarrail's command was back on Greek territory by mid-December.

The Austro-Hungarian army attacked the Montenegrins around Mojkovac on 5 January 1916 and while their successful defence helped the Serbian army escape, they eventually surrendered on 25 January. Their defeat meant that Germany could finally open their coveted railway link to the Ottoman Empire. The Austro-Hungarians then pushed the Italians out of Albania, forcing the Allies to withdraw into neutral Greece.

The Allies had dug a fortified position around the port of Thessaloniki, where they were eventually joined by the Serbian army. The Germans attacked on 17 August 1916, clearing the area east of the River Struma, but a counter-attack on 12 September captured the important Kaymakchalan peak on Nidže Mountain. The Bulgarian occupation of eastern Macedonia and the surrender of a large number of troops to a small German force sparked a coup in Greece. It resulted in anti-royalist officers taking control of Thessaloniki and Macedonia.

The allied *Armée d'Orient* received reinforcements over the winter but their April attack still failed, resulting in further unrest across Greece. The king's supporters wanted to withdraw from the war, so the Allies blockaded the Greek ports. An ultimatum then led to the king abdicating in favour of his second son, Alexander, which united the Greeks. The country also backed a return of Prime Minister Eleftherios Venizelos and his decisive declaration of war against the Central Powers.

Bulgarian and Austrian forces put an end to a Serbian uprising around Toplica in March 1917. The Macedonian front then remained stable until the autumn of 1918, when the German and Austro-Hungarian armies began to withdraw. French and Serbian troops broke though the Bulgarian lines at Dobro Pole in September 1918 but they fought back against the British and Greeks around Dojran. Bulgaria eventually surrendered on 29 September 1918 and the Allied forces were able to advance both north-west towards Vienna and north-east towards Budapest.

The Austro-Hungarian Empire would be divided up after the Great War and the new Kingdom of Serbs, Croats and Slovenes was given a large part of Hungary under the Treaty of Trianon. The new nation may have been dominated by the Serbs but the people had suffered horrendous casualties, both military and civilian. Reported losses were so high that the Bulgarian Prime Minister, Vasil Radoslavov, announced that 'Serbia [had] ceased to exist' in 1917. Around one million Serb soldiers had died, half of them engaged, the other half from starvation and disease, many of them during a typhus epidemic in 1915.

Albania during the Great War

Albania had gained its independence from the Ottoman Empire back in November 1912 and the new nation had been recognised under the Treaty of London which had been signed in May 1913. The principality had been established in February 1914 and the German prince William of Wied had been pronounced its king. However, problems between the ethnic groups resulted in an uprising, which was organised by Essad Pasha and financed by Italy in May. Pasha ended up being arrested and sentenced to death, but he escaped to Italy and Haxhi Qamili took over the pro-Turkish rebellion.

Italy had always wanted the port of Vlorë on the Albanian coast, as part of its plan to establish a foothold in the Balkans. So Rome supported a coup which ended with Turhan Përmeti taking control of Albania. A revolt around Tirana followed, but the outbreak of the Great War ended the stand-off. Italy moved troops into Albania, staking its claim before the Austro-Hungarian Empire could, but William of Wied declared the country's neutrality first. The local chiefs responded by rejecting the Protocol of Corfu and they seized control of Albania before driving Prince William into exile.

The Allies agreed Greek troops could occupy northern Epirus in October 1914, but they were also anxious to secure Italian support. So they promised Rome would form a protectorate over part of the area under the secret Treaty of London in April 1915. The treaty also promised the north of the country to Serbia and Montenegro, while the south would be given to Greece. Albania was divided between the three countries in the autumn of 1915.

The German and Austro-Hungarian Empires launched a combined offensive against Serbia on 7 October 1915. The Bulgarian armies joined in two weeks later, helping to drive the Serbian armies across Albania. The evacuation of 150,000 Serbs to the Greek island of Corfu was complete by February 1916. The Austro-Hungarian and Bulgarian armies could then occupy Albania, and Ahmed Zogu was allowed to establish an administration in February 1916 while Essad Pasha was forced into exile.

Italian troops occupied southern Albania in the summer 1916 and French troops moved into the Korçë area in the autumn; they then advanced side-by-side into northern Epirus. The French formed the Albanian Republic of Korçë, while the Austro-Hungarian Empire declared Albania was its protectorate. The Italians then declared Albania was under its protection in June 1916 and moved more troops in, against the wishes of Great Britain and France. Rome planned to expand its zone of protection across northern Greece and western Macedonia when the Central Powers collapsed in the autumn 1918.

The Serbs also moved up the Albanian coast as far as the Struma River and they joined the Allied assault against the Bulgarian army. The Central Powers were driven north of Thessaloniki in September 1918, which forced the Austro-Hungarians to abandon Albania. The war may have been over but four armies occupied Albania. Serbian troops held the mountains in the north; Greek troops held a small area in the south; French troops held Korçë and Shkodër; Italian troops held the rest of the country.

The Treaty of London may have promised Albania to Italy but the Allies changed their mind because the Italian armies had contributed so little to the war effort. The new plan was to divide the northern part of Albania between Serbia and Montenegro, while the south was given to Greece. The Albanians, however, were determined to remain independent and their politicians announced a provisional government during the Durrës Congress in December 1918. The Italian troops would be driven out in the summer of 1920 in what was called the Vlorë War. The United States would support Albania's independence and it would be admitted to the League of Nations at the end of 1920.

Bulgaria during the Great War

Bulgaria had lost most of the lands it had gained in the First Balkan War after the Second Balkan War. The loss of Southern Dobruja had resulted in a drastic cut in grain production and a poor harvest had increased the food shortages. These problems occurred while the country was being forced to accept 120,000 refugees from Serbian and Greek areas.

Bulgaria had wanted to make friends after the Second Balkan War but the Central Powers had kept their distance. Great Britain and France had let Russia deal with Bulgaria. Initially, they all refused to lend any money to help it boost its frail economy and buy in food. Eventually, Berlin offered a huge loan in July 1914 in return for control of Bulgaria's mining and construction projects. The agreement resulted in arguments in the Bulgarian parliament, but they ended following the assassination of Archduke Franz Ferdinand.

The Austro-Hungarian Empire had declared war on Serbia on 28 July 1914 but Bulgaria had remained neutral as the conflict spread quickly across Europe. Instead, it focused on building up its army while martial law kept the peace. Sofia even remained neutral after the Ottoman Empire joined the Central Powers in October 1914, despite a mutual defence treaty with Constantinople. It also refused the Entente's offer of extra territories if it remained neutral for the duration of the war.

Prime Minister Vasil Radoslavov was waiting to see how the war played out, so Bulgaria could join the winning side and gain as much territory as possible. The Allied invasion of Gallipoli in April 1915 and Italy's siding with the Entente a month later increased the Balkans' importance. The Allies may have promised Bulgaria more territory if it attacked the Ottoman Empire, while the Germans demanded repayments for their recent loan, but Radoslavov still refused to join either side.

Events then turned against the Allies, because Italy was struggling against the Austro-Hungarian Empire, while the Russians came under pressure on the Eastern Front and the Gallipoli expedition faltered. This time it was Germany who was offering Bulgaria territories if it joined the Central Powers, but Radoslavov again refused.

Both the Entente and the Central Powers continued to offer bribes to Bulgaria through the summer of 1915. The Entente wanted to support Serbia and give Russia assistance, neutralising the Ottoman threat. Meanwhile the Central Powers wanted Serbia out of the war, to separate Russia from the rest of the Entente. It would also give them an overland route to supply the Ottomans.

Bulgaria eventually joined the Central Powers under the Treaty of Amity and Alliance, which was signed on 6 September 1915. A public promise of a large loan and a secret promise of new territories had convinced Radoslavov to join. The Central Powers' plan was for Germany and the Austro-Hungarians to attack Serbia in a month's time, with Bulgaria following just five days later. Bulgaria started mobilising its army and while the Entente presented an ultimatum threatening war, all it could do was land a small force in Salonika. Bulgarian troops would invade Serbian territory on 14 October, undermining the Allied position on the Gallipoli peninsula.

The Bulgarian Army

The Bulgarian Army had recently demobilised following the Second Balkan War and while it had been left with only 65,000 regular soldiers, it had another 300,000 men in its reserve and a similar number of men in the militia. Minister of War, Major General Nikola Zhekov, had been appointed commander-in-chief of the Bulgaria army, but its mobilisation had to be postponed until 22 September 1915 to give Colonel Petar Ganchev time to visit Germany and discuss an alliance. Two armies then deployed on the Serbian border, while a third assembled on the Romanian border, bringing the total number of soldiers deployed to 600,000.

The Conquest of Serbia

The Austro-Hungarian Empire asked for help to defeat the Serbians, so the Germans sent an army to help it in the autumn of 1915. General August von Mackensen launched his attack across the Sava and Danube Rivers on 6 October 1915, expecting the Bulgarians to attack a few days later. Serbia had divided its armies between its northern and eastern borders but the delay to the Bulgarian mobilisation had given them time to deploy its reserves against the more serious northern attack.

Two Bulgarian armies eventually crossed the Serbian border on 14 October. One army encountered stiff resistance in the hills beyond the Morava valley, before the winter weather set in. Meanwhile, the other army split in two as it advanced across Vardar Macedonia; half would drive the Serbs out of Skopje while the rest had to face the French task force moving north to meet it.

Bulgarian troops captured the Serbs' wartime capital, Niš, on 5 November, and they linked with the German troops advancing south. They focused on General Maurice Sarrail's small force and it fell back after Pristina fell on 23 November. The French and British were then driven back past Dojran and across the Greek border, while the Serb force escaped into the Albanian mountains. Around 50,000 Serb soldiers and civilians succumbed to the winter conditions but 130,000 escaped. Over 35,000 Bulgarian soldiers had lost their lives clearing Vardar Macedonia.

The Vardar front was eventually broken in September 1918 and it forced Tsar Ferdinand to sue for a humiliating peace. The Bulgarian armies had to surrender their weapons and leave Serbian and Greek territories. All German and Austrian troops had to leave Bulgaria while Allied troops garrisoned strategic points across the country. The people of Bulgaria demonstrated against the shame, while Aleksandar Stamboliyski, leader of the Agrarian National Union, persuaded the unpopular Ferdinand to abdicate. His son, Boris III, was appointed Tsar while the army restored peace across Bulgaria, before it demobilised.

Greece in the Great War

Greece had been on the victorious side in the two Balkan Wars, resulting in the nation doubling the size of its territories, at the expense of Bulgaria and the Ottoman Empire. Meanwhile, Bulgaria was seeking revenge against Serbia and Greece, so the two countries signed a pact of mutual assistance in June 1913. The Ottoman Empire was also unhappy and it claimed its lost Aegean islands before driving the ethnic Greeks from Anatolia over the spring and summer of 1914. The Serbians refused to get involved, while the Greek generals advised against invading Anatolia because it would leave the country vulnerable to attack by Bulgaria.

A Greek amphibious landing on the Gallipoli peninsula was being considered when Archduke Franz Ferdinand was assassinated in Sarajevo on 28 June 1914. All talk of attacking the Ottoman Empire ceased and Greeks were left deciding what to do as Europe moved towards war. The Greeks' dilemma was whether they should join the Entente or remain neutral. But Athens knew it would have been unwise to join the Central Powers because the British Royal Navy would be able to blockade the nation's ports.

King Constantine had been educated in Germany and Queen Sofia was the Kaiser's sister. The nation's armed forces were also pro–German because they had been trained by German officers. However, Greece had signed a mutual defence pact with Serbia to protect itself against Bulgaria, and the Austro-Hungarian Empire had attacked Serbia at the beginning of the conflict.

The conflict of interests had led to a National Schism in which the king wanted Greece to stay out of the war while the Prime Minister, Eleftherios Venizelos, had wanted to take the Allied side. Venizelos advised Constantine to take up the British offer of Ottoman territories if Greece joined the Entente, but he refused. Venizelos would be forced to resign, only to be reinstated when his party won the June 1915 election.

The Serbs asked for help but Prime Minister Venizelos decided against doing so, as the conflict spread across Europe. He also refused to join the Germans and instead sought advice from the Entente. Britain thought Greece should stay neutral as long as the Ottoman Empire remained neutral. However, both France and Russia failed to reply because they wanted Bulgaria to join the Entente and that involved bribing Sofia with Greek territories. Greece's stance was then challenged when the Ottoman Empire joined the Central Powers in October 1914.

Greece ignored Serbia's pleas for help for a second time in December and rejected Britain's request to join the Entente the following month. Venizelos then discovered that Germany was paying Bulgaria so it could move supplies across its territories to Constantinople. However, he dared not join the Entente in case the move provoked Bulgaria, leaving Greece facing a two-front war.

The balance of power in the Eastern Mediterranean changed when the Allies sent a naval task force to the Aegean Sea in February 1915 with plans to sail through the Dardanelle Straits to threaten Constantinople. Venizelos offered Greek military assistance, against General Ioannis Metaxas's advice, and they both resigned. Venizelos would return as Prime Minister after winning a June election.

The Allied warships were unable to get through the Dardanelle Straits. They made an amphibious landing on the Gallipoli peninsula on 25 April 1915, but it resulted in deadlock. Little had changed by the time Bulgaria allied with Germany at the beginning of September 1915.

Venizelos finally declared Greece would join the Entente but it would take time to mobilise the army because of a shortage of transport. Athens' situation changed significantly when Bulgaria declared war on Serbia in October 1915. The defence pact with Serbia was updated while Venizelos called for Greece to declare war on Bulgaria which resulted in him having to resign for a second time.

Venizelos's confidential plea for Allied help resulted in two divisions (one British and one French) being diverted from Gallipoli to Thessaloniki. However, no one had told Athens and there was a stand-off as the ships were denied access to the harbour. The Allies pretended they needed to land troops to secure a link with the Serbs and they landed after a half-hearted protest by the Greek government. A furious King Constantine would sack Venizelos for deepening Greece's involvement in the war.

The new prime minister, Alexandros Zaimis, announced Greece could not help Serbia, even after it was attacked by Austrian and German troops on 7 October 1915. Bulgaria joined in only a week later and the combined armies drove the Serbian army back into Albania.

General Maurice Sarrail organised the 75,000 French troops at Thessaloniki into the Armée d'Orient while General Bryan Mahon organised a similar number of men into the Salonika Force. The Allied counter-attack failed but the Bulgarians continued advancing to Skopje, driving a wedge between the Allied forces and the Serbs. The Allies had to withdraw towards Thessaloniki, while the Serbs were driven back to the Adriatic Coast.

The Salonica Front

Stefanos Skouloudis replaced Alexandros Zaimis as prime minister after only a few weeks. The Allies were dismayed when Greece's new prime minister announced that the Allied troops would be disarmed if they re-entered Greek territory. A compromise was struck in which the Allies were allowed to create a fortified camp around Thessaloniki while the Greeks occupied the port itself. They also deployed troops across eastern Macedonia, to face the Bulgarians.

The German Chief of the General Staff, General Erich von Falkenhayn, demanded that both the Allied and then Serbian troops left Greece. He threatened to invade if Athens did not withdraw its troops from Macedonia and allow German troops to enter its territory. As the Greeks considered the demands, the Allies were busy evacuating the surviving Serbian troops from the Albania coast to Corfu.

Around 130,000 Serbian soldiers were eventually shipped to the mainland over the winter, where they were armed and ready to fight again. They joined the Allied forces in Macedonia and advanced towards the Greek frontier on 12 March 1916. The Germans and Bulgarians countered the move, only to discover that the Greek troops had instructions not to engage them. Only Major General Andreas Bairas ignored the order; he held onto Fort Rupel in Central Macedonia until Athens ordered him to abandon it on 25 May.

The Bulgarians advanced across eastern Macedonia, sparking a crisis in which the Greek army began demobilising. There was also a mass exodus from the area as tens of thousands tried to escape Bulgarian atrocities. The Allies eventually had to impose martial law in Thessaloniki and take over the harbour to safeguard their supply route.

The Allies were preparing to attack in Macedonia when the Germans and Bulgarians launched their own on 17 August 1916. Prime Minister Zaimis's request for financial aid was ignored, so the Greek army put up no resistance. All the Allies could do was blockade Kavala harbour to the east of Thessaloniki. Then, after two years of neutrality, Romania saw its chance to take on its old enemy, Bulgaria: Bucharest declared it was joining the war on the Allied side.

Greece became even more divided as the months passed, as the National Schism split the country into two factions. Officers who supported Venizelos had been plotting an attack against Bulgaria and their Committee of National Defence staged a short-lived revolt on 30 August 1916. The Bulgarians took advantage of the confusing situation by trapping an entire corps in eastern Macedonia.

The monarchists blamed Allied interference for Greece's troubles while the government supporters increased their calls to join the Allies. Meanwhile, the Allies suspected that the Greeks had staged the revolt in cooperation with the Central Powers. As the politicians argued, Venizelos had to set up a Provisional Government of National Defence to quell the riots on the streets.

The revolution in Russia and the abdication of Tsar Nicholas II in March 1917 left King Constantine without any supporters in the Allied camp. The loss of eastern Macedonia had led to officers dividing into the pro-Venizelos group, who called themselves the National Defence, and the pro-royalist group, who were known as the Reservists.

The Allies were even more desperate to get Greece into the war, so they established a naval blockade after Venizelos' supporters stopped the Greek fleet going to sea. Events eventually came to a head in June 1917 when Allied warships threatened to shell Athens. King Constantine was driven into exile. He took his eldest son, George, leaving his second son, Alexander, behind to be crowned. The young king would be kept in isolation while his supporters were either imprisoned or exiled. After three long years, Venizelos finally got his wish when Greece declared war against the Central Powers on 30 June 1917.

The Macedonian Front would remain stable until the Greeks defeated the Bulgarians at the Battle of Skra-di-Legen on 30 May 1918. The Bulgarians made no attempt to recover any lost ground, because they had lost the will to fight. Prime Minister Radoslavov was forced to resign, while everyone blamed him for getting Bulgaria into debt and for taking the decision to join the Central Powers. His replacement, Aleksandar Malinov, secretly offered to sign an armistice if Bulgaria was allowed to keep part of Macedonia. The British Prime Minister, David Lloyd George, refused.

Both sides spent the summer reinforcing their armies and General Franchet d'Espèrey took command of the French task force. The Allies eventually attacked on 15 September and a prolonged bombardment made sure the French, Greek and Serb force was able to drive the Bulgarians back. British and Greek attacks around Doiran Lake were defeated on

18 September but a breakthrough at Dobro Pole forced the Bulgarians to abandon the Vardar Mountains. A general withdrawal followed and Skopje fell on 29 September 1918, the day Bulgaria signed the Armistice of Salonica.

Around 5,000 Bulgarian deserters turned on their commanders before taking control of the railway hub of Radomir. Members of the Agrarian National Union then took control of the mutineers and they marched on Sofia on 28 September. They also declared an end to the Bulgarian monarchy and the beginning of a new republic. This time a request for an armistice was accepted, bringing the fighting across Macedonia to an end on 30 September. Bulgarian troops were able to stop the rebellion but Tsar Ferdinand still abdicated and went into exile.

British troops were heading east towards Constantinople when the Armistice of Mudros was signed with the Ottoman Empire on 26 October. Meanwhile, French and Serbian troops were marching into Albania, Montenegro and Serbia when the Austro-Hungarian Empire signed an armistice on the Italian Front on 3 November. The Hungarians signed the Armistice of Belgrade a week later, just hours before the general armistice across Europe came into force on 11 November.

The Treaty of Sèvres would hand Western Thrace to Greece, depriving Bulgaria of its access to the Aegean Sea. It also took Eastern Thrace from Turkey, removing its final foothold from mainland Europe, and awarded it to Greece. The area around Smyrna, on Anatolia, was also handed to Greece, giving it a port on the east side of the Aegean Sea.

Romania in the Great War

King Carol wanted Romania to join the Central Powers but the nation's political parties preferred to join the Triple Entente. Only Carol had signed a secret pre-war treaty with the Entente, which would not allow Bucharest to go to war unless the Austro-Hungarian Empire came under attack first. It left Romania stuck in a neutral position because it attacked Serbia first.

The British Secretary of State for War, Field Marshal Earl Horatio Kitchener, sent Lieutenant Colonel Christopher Thomson to Bucharest in 1915 to assess Romania's potential. He believed it would be dangerous to sign it up as a new ally but his advice was ignored. Bucharest would sign a treaty with the Allies in August 1916, which agreed it would declare war on the Austro-Hungarian Empire at the end of the month. Germany, Bulgaria and the Ottoman Empire responded with their own declarations of war, leaving Bucharest in the position it had wanted to avoid; a war on two fronts.

Romania may have had a large army but its 650,000 soldiers had been given limited training and units were short of weapons and ammunition. The Allies then had to consider a new danger because the Germans would try seize the Ploieşti oilfields, north of Bucharest. All London could do was to order Colonel Thomson to help the Romanian engineers disable the wells.

Romania wanted to add Transylvania to its territory, so three armies crossed its north-west border on 27 August 1916 and began driving the Austro-Hungarians back. To begin with, the 'Z Hypothesis' plan was successful and the advancing troops were welcomed by the ethnic Romanians. However, Berlin immediately sent General Falkenhayn to Transylvania and his troops had soon stopped the offensive.

Field Marshal August von Mackensen's mixed army of Bulgarian, German and Ottoman troops crossed Romania's southern border and besieged Turtucaia on the River Danube. The huge fortress was sometimes referred to as the 'Verdun of the East'; a reference to France's famous fortress which had withstood weeks of prolonged attacks. However, this siege only lasted five days and the Romanian armies were soon in full retreat.

The British and French promised to launch a counter-attack against the Macedonian front to draw the Bulgarian's attention to their southern border, only it never materialised. Meanwhile Russian assurances to send reinforcements also turned out to be hollow, because too few divisions were sent to make a difference. It left Romania facing the combined might of the Central Powers' armies on two long fronts.

A counter-attack had stopped the Transylvania offensive by 15 September 1916, and a few days later the Romanian attack defeated the Bulgarians at Cobadin. An attempt to send troops across the River Danube to attack the German rear had to be called off because Falkenhayn launched his own counterattack. His armies drove the Romanians back through the Carpathian Mountains as far as the River Jiu. A second German attack on 1 November 1916 soon reached the River Olt, while a third cleared the Vulcan Pass.

Meanwhile, Mackensen and the Bulgarian general Stefan Toshev had launched their own combined offensive through Constanţa and Dobruja on 19 October. A month later they had a bridgehead across the Danube and were soon following up the Romanians as they fell back towards Bucharest. General Constantin Prezan attempted to protect the capital but the Russians gave no support and it was lost a few days later. The whole of Southern Romania may have fallen to the Central Powers soon afterwards but the winter weather brought campaigning to a halt in the Carpathian Mountains.

The Romanian armies may have suffered around 250,000 casualties, but the survivors still reorganised and managed to train tens of thousands of new conscripts throughout the first half of 1917. An improved logistics system meant that the weapons and ammunition sent by the British and French could be delivered to the front line.

The Romanian High Command promised Moscow it would attack in support of the Kerensky Offensive which the Russians planned to launch in July. However, the Germans and Austro-Hungarians attacked first in Moldavia, resulting in fierce battles west of the River Danube. The Romanians were getting the upper hand, advancing between the Eastern Carpathians and the Black Sea, until the Kerensky Offensive failed. It allowed the Central Powers to divert reserves from the Russian front, and Army Group Mackensen was ready to counter-attack on 6 August. Nearly one million Central Powers troops would try again and again to break the Romanian line, until their offensive was called off on 3 September.

Romania may have held its own, but events beyond its control were about to lead to its downfall. The October Revolution (which occurred in November under the New Style Calendar) led to a civil war across Russia, depriving the Romanians of their closest ally. Isolated and outnumbered, they had to agree to the Focşani Armistice, which was signed on 9 December 1917.

The Central Powers demanded that Romania agree to sign the Treaty of Bucharest in May 1918, and it did, despite King Ferdinand's refusal. The Germans appointed Alexandru Marghiloman as the country's prime minister and then sent engineers to Ploieşti to repair the oil wells. Great efforts were then made to export huge amounts of grain and oil to Germany. The fresh source of food and fuel meant the German armed forces could keep fighting on the Western Front through the summer and autumn.

Bulgaria went out of the war when the Armistice of Salonica was signed on 30 September 1918 and the Ottoman Empire followed under the Armistice of Mudros on 30 October. Romania would re-enter the war on the Allied side on 10 November 1918, the day before the war in Europe ended. The Treaty of Bucharest was reversed under the Armistice and both the Austro-Hungarian Empire and Bulgaria had to return territories to Romania.

The map of the Balkans was redrawn after the Great War, with Romania gaining territory at the expense of its neighbours. Communism in the USSR and fascism in Italy were on the borders of the Balkans.

Chapter 3

Recovering from the War

December 1918 to October 1929

The Treaty of Trianon and the Little Entente

The Treaty of Versailles ended the state of war between the Allies and Germany in June 1919 and the Treaty of Saint-Germain-en-Laye did the same for Austria three months later. The Treaty of Trianon would end the war between most of the Allies and Hungary in June 1920 but Budapest faced having to pay huge reparations for being part of the Central Powers. The treaty divided up the Austro-Hungarian Empire, because the new, smaller nations would be easier to control. It would also deprive Germany of their united support in the future.

Hungary had to hand over most of its territories to Czechoslovakia, Romania and the Kingdom of the Slovenes, Croats and Serbs. It left the country just a quarter of its pre-war size, with only one third of its pre-war population and little of its industry still in its hands. Five of Hungary's cities were in other countries, its rail network had been cut and it had lost its access to the Adriatic Sea. Unemployment rose as industry and agriculture struggled to reassert themselves, while imports and exports fell due to prejudices against Hungary. The combination of factors left Budapest trying to balance a weak economy which was vulnerable to outside influences.

Hungary's armed forces also had to be reduced to a minimum. Its army was reduced to only 35,000 men and conscription was banned, leaving only enough men to keep the peace. Artillery units were stripped of their guns, tanks were banned and the air force was disbanded because planes were forbidden.

The Great War and the Treaty of Trianon had a huge negative impact on the Balkans. Economies had been devastated and settlements destroyed, presenting economic challenges as nations came to terms with what industries they had been left with. The fighting had caused enormous casualties across the region; for example, 1.5 million Serbs, or one in four of the population, had died in the fighting or from disease. The conflict had also left the area very short of horses and mules.

The breaking up of the Austro-Hungarian and Ottoman Empires changed borders, with the countries which had fought alongside the Allies gaining territories at the expense of those who had supported the Central Powers. It resulted in millions living in countries where their language, religion and culture were not recognised, resulting in ethnic tensions. Hundreds of thousands were forcibly moved from their homes, while many more chose to leave to escape the discrimination, creating resentment that would last for decades.

The Hungarian armed forces may have been cut back but there were fears that Budapest would reform them to reclaim its territories. So the three countries signed defence treaties to protect themselves under what became known as the Little Entente (as opposed to the Triple Entente, the pre-war treaty signed by Great Britain, France and Russia). The three countries' fears were realised when Charles I of Austria tried to seize the Hungarian throne in 1921. They had to mobilise their armies until he was arrested and had his sovereign rights stripped from him.

Timeline of the 1920s across the Balkans

December 1918	The Kingdom of Serbs, Croats and Slovenes is formed
May 1919	Greek troops invade Anatolia
June 1919	The Treaty of Versailles ends the state of war between the Allies and Germany
September 1919	The Treaty of Saint-Germain-en-Laye ends the state of war between the Allies and Austria
November 1919	Bulgaria hands over large territories under the Treaty of Neuilly
June 1920	The Treaty of Trianon ends the state of war between the Allies and Hungary
August 1920	The Treaty of Sèvres gives Greece extra territories
September 1920	Albania drives out Italian troops in the Vlorë War
June 1921	The Kingdom of Serbs, Croats and Slovenes passes the Vidovdan Constitution
1921 and 1922	Czechoslovakia, Romania and the Kingdom of Serbs, Croats and Slovenes sign the Little Entente

August 1922	A Turkish counter-attack drives the Greeks back
October 1922	The Allies and the Ottomans signed the Armistice of Mudanya
October 1922	The National Fascist Party seize power of Italy
September 1923	Communist uprisings across Bulgaria
March 1924	Greece declares the Second Hellenic Republic
1926 and 1927	Albania signs treaties with Italy
1928	President Ahmet Bej Zogu is declared King Zog of the Albanians
October 1929	The Wall Street Crash triggers the Great Depression, reducing trade and industrial output while increasing unemployment and economic difficulties

The Kingdom of Serbs, Croats and Slovenes in the 1920s

The Slavs wanted the Slovenes, the Croats and the Serbs bringing together into an independent state. In July 1917, Serb Nikola Pašić and Croat Ante Trumbić agreed to work together to create one state headed by the exiled King Petar I. The Kingdom of Serbs, Croats and Slovenes came into being on 1 December 1918, uniting the South Slav peoples; Trumbić would represent them at the Versailles Peace Conference.

There were problems forming a government as the new nation came to terms with its mixture of people and religions. Ljubomir Davidović was eventually appointed prime minister and his Democratic Party ruled by decree (using temporary laws), only for the King to stop him holding elections. Stojan Protić's Parliamentary Community then took control but it too was forced to rule by decree. Strikes eventually forced the Democratic Party and the Radical Party to compromise over centralisation and land reform. Milenko Vesnić was appointed prime minister but members of the Croatian Republican Peasant Party refused to swear allegiance to the King. They also refused to take their seats in parliament, as did most of the other opposition members. Even so, the Vidovdan Constitution (named after the Serbian holiday of Saint Vitus) was passed in June 1921, making the Kingdom of Serbs, Croats and Slovenes into a united monarchy.

The Kingdom of Serbs, Croats and Slovenes started life with many problems, starting with the death of King Petar only two months after its creation; he was replaced by his son, Alexander. It had begun its existence in huge financial debt to the West, with little hope of paying it off, and the interest payments crippled the budget. Most of the population were engaged in agriculture and the economy would struggle on until it was devastated by the effects of the Great Depression which followed the Wall Street Crash of October 1929.

The ethnic tension between the Serbs, Croats, Slovenes, Bosnians, Macedonians and Albanians soon became apparent. The Serbs dominated the nation's politics, but the Croat Republican Peasant Party and the Croatian Party of Rights fought back by calling for equality, with a view to getting an independent Croatian state. The Croatian parties formed the Croatian National Representation in 1921, only to throw the Party of Rights out the following year. The group may have opposed Serbian nationalism, but that did not stop it secretly working with the pro-Serb People's Radical Party, with the aim of organising a rebellion to break up the kingdom.

The Albanian community faced many prejudices because they did not speak Serbo-Croatian. The Kingdom had a mixture of religions to contend with and state laws favoured the dominant Roman Catholics in the north and the Orthodox Catholics in the south over their Muslim Bosniak neighbours.

The Kingdom of Serbs, Croats and Slovenes also had issues with its new neighbours. A referendum placed Carinthia under Austrian rule, while the Treaty of Rapallo placed the one million Slovenes living around Trieste under Italian rule. The Dalmatian port of Zadar and the City of Rijeka (called Fiume by the Italians) were also transferred. Tensions would increase between Belgrade and Rome when Mussolini's National Fascist Party seized power in Italy in October 1922.

Serbian Nikola Pašić declared the Peasant's Party a security threat at the end of 1924, so Stjepan Radić and his team were imprisoned, with the King's approval. The rest of the party members boycotted parliament, which increased its popularity, but the February 1925 election was rigged in the Serbs' favour. The arguments culminated with the Serb deputy Puniša Račić shooting five members of the Croatian Peasant Party while parliament was sitting on 20 June 1928. Stjepan Radić died a few days later and the surviving Croatian deputies again withdrew from parliament. They called for the 1 December 1920 declaration of the founding of the Kingdom of Serbs, Croats and Slovenes to be replaced with one which gave them equality.

King Alexander I took action against the Croatian nationalist organisations in August 1928 by having their senior members arrested. Many Croat activists chose to go into exile in Italy, where Ante Pavelić would organise them into a paramilitary organisation with fascist and nationalist ideals. The Ustaša Croatian Revolutionary Movement (usually referred to as the Ustaše) would train, ready to strike back in their homeland when the time was right.

One of those arrested was Josip Broz, the committee secretary for a Zagreb trade union. The young Broz had fought in the Austro–Hungarian army, first against the Serbs and then on the Russian front in 1914. He was captured early in 1915 and would embrace pro-Bolshevik politics as he recovered from his wounds. Broz would serve in a Red Guard unit during the October Revolution before he returned to his native Croatia. He joined the Communists, promoting his politics through the local trade union after the Party was forbidden.

King Alexander eventually decided the only way to take control of the Kingdom of Serbs, Croats and Slovenes was to close its parliament and ban the political parties on 6 January 1929. The Constitution was abolished and the name Kingdom of Yugoslavia, or the Land of the Southern Slavs, was adopted. The country was reorganised from thirty-three *oblasts*, or regions, into nine *banovinas*, or provinces, to simplify the running of the country. The king also established a Court for the Protection of the State to stop opposition to his monarchy.

Albania in the 1920s

The Treaty of London had promised central and southern Albania to Italy as a reward for joining the Entente in the Great War. Italian soldiers had occupied the area in the autumn of 1916 and it had been declared a protectorate in June 1917. However, the Allies considered Italy had contributed little to their cause. Both the British and French had been forced to send reinforcements to the Italian front following its collapse during the battle of Caporetto in October 1917. As a result, the Allies defaulted on their promise and announced the creation of the state of Albania; a delegation was permitted to attend the Paris Peace Conference.

The First National Assembly may have accepted Italian protection and an Italian prince but a Second National Assembly rejected a suggestion from France, Britain and Greece to split Albania up. Instead, a regency and parliament were established in Tirana, the country's new capital. The Italian troops were eventually driven out in September 1920 in what was known as the Vlorë War. The League of Nations supported Albania, so Rome gave up its claim in the Balkans, only for it to be resurrected by Benito Mussolini when his National Fascist Party seized power in 1922.

Albania also faced arguments with its neighbours over their borders. The Kingdom of Serbs, Croats and Slovenes supported the clan chief, Gjon Markagjoni, when he established the Mirdita Republic. The League of Nations became involved when Yugoslav troops invaded Albania in November 1921 and Markagjoni's republic was dissolved when the new border was set.

The Popular Party formed a government in December 1921, the first of many, because control of Albania was being fought over by wealthy landowners and clan leaders. The country had no banking system, little infrastructure and few industries but it did have lots of peasants struggling to farm the land without machinery. It was also a country divided by religion, with the Christians wanting the area to break free from its Islamic past. All these problems left the government struggling to assert the nation's independence in the 1920s.

Prime Minister Ahmet Zogu became involved in three scandals in quick succession. The first involved him quitting the Popular Party after becoming engaged to the daughter of the Progressive Party leader, Shefqet Vërlaci. The second came when he ended the engagement, making an enemy of the country's wealthiest landowner in a country renowned for its blood feuds. A member of the republican National Union (*Bashkimi Kombëtar*) injured Zogu during a failed assassination attempt in 1924, so he retaliated by having the party's leader, Avni Rustemi, murdered. Zogu was then implicated in a financial scandal and he went into exile after peasants seized control of Tirana in June 1924.

Bishop Fan Noli was appointed prime minister and while mercenaries were recruited to secure the borders, plans were introduced to modernise Albania. Noli may have sentenced Zogu to death in his absence but Zogu returned with a Serbian-backed army in December and seized control of Tirana. This time it was Noli who had to leave the country, as Zogu was re-elected prime minister in January 1925. He handed over territory to the Kingdom of Serbs, Croats and Slovenes for supporting his return to power, only for Belgrade to then refuse to work with Albania.

Tirana started accepting financial loans from Italy and Zogu agreed to deal exclusively with Rome under the First Treaty of Tirana in November 1926. A second treaty invited Italian officers to train the Albanian military, but it was a dangerous partnership because Mussolini was looking to take over the country to establish a foothold in the Balkans.

President Ahmet Bej Zogu, as he had become in 1925, was declared king of the Albanians in 1928 and he chose to use the non-Arabic title

King Zog to make himself more appealing to European Christian countries. A new assembly took control from the senate and elections were banned, allowing Zog's supporters to run Albania with an iron fist. Civil liberties were often denied, while political opponents were arrested in what was effectively a royal dictatorship. The police state then seized power from the local landowners (known as *beys*) so it could be centralised, making Albania a united nation under Zog's rule.

Zog replaced Albania's ancient Islamic legal system with a modern version. He also sought to minimise the influence of the Christian and Islamic churches, to prevent them becoming influential in the new nation's politics. His aim was to unite the people through patriotism, rather than allow them to be divided by religion.

Bulgaria in the 1920s

Bulgaria was forced to hand over a large part of its territories in November 1919 under the Treaty of Neuilly. Macedonia was given to the Kingdom of Serbs, Croats and Slovenes, Dobruja was given to Romania, and Thrace's Aegean coast was given to Greece. The huge loss of territory caused much resentment, particularly amongst those forced to live in another country.

Aleksandar Stamboliyski's Agrarian Party won the March 1920 elections but it soon found it difficult to pay the reparations it owed to the Kingdom of Serbs, Croats and Slovenes and Romania. An agreement setting the border with Kingdom of Serbs, Croats and Slovenes was signed in March 1923 but a right-wing coalition headed by Aleksander Tsankov seized control of Bulgaria just three months later. The Internal Macedonian Revolutionary Organisation (IMRO) would later murder Stamboliyski for giving up Bulgaria's claim to Macedonia.

The Bulgarian Communist Party initially stayed out of political arguments because it viewed them as a struggle between the urban and rural bourgeoisie. However, calls for an uprising by Georgi Dimitrov and Vasil Kolarov resulted in 2,000 Communist Party members being arrested on 12 September 1923. Demonstrations across the country inspired the communists' Central Committee to launch an uprising on 23 September, starting with an armed insurrection in north-west Bulgaria. Meanwhile, the Sophia committee chose to take legal action, only for its members to be arrested. It left the army able to focus on the rural uprising and 800 were killed in the fighting that followed. The uprising was crushed and the surviving rebels, including Georgi Dimitrov and Vasil Kolarov, went into exile.

The country remained unstable and further crackdowns had to be introduced in 1925 after two failed assassination attempts against Tsar Boris III. Tsankov would eventually resign the following year, leaving Andrey Lyapchev's moderate government to take control of Bulgaria.

Romania in the 1920s

Romania was given a huge amount of territory as a reward for helping the Allies during the Great War. The Romanian National Assembly proclaimed the union with Transylvania on its north-west border in December 1918. The addition of Bukovina to its northern border would be approved under the Treaty of Saint-Germain-en-Laye in September 1919. However, the rest of the territories were not handed over so readily.

Mihály Károlyi was appointed Hungary's new prime minister when the Austro-Hungarian Empire collapsed at the end of the Great War. Its huge army was reduced in size as Czechoslovak, Serbian and Romanian troops moved in to occupy the confiscated areas. It reduced Hungary to just a quarter of its pre-war size. The Paris Peace Conference may have agreed a temporary border between Hungary and Romania in February 1919 but the Károlyi government refused to withdraw Hungarian troops from the area.

Béla Kun staged a successful coup in March 1919 (only days after he was released from prison) and declared Hungary a Soviet Republic as the communists took control of the government. The communist vision may have been accepted in urban areas but harsh measures, called the Red Terror, had to be implemented to bring the rural areas into line.

The Romanians asked the Paris Peace Conference for permission to oust Kun's government but it chose to send the South African politician General Jan Smuts to Bucharest instead. Kun refused to accept his suggestions and mobilised the Hungarian Red Army to reoccupy the lost territories. Their attack in April 1919 failed but the Romanians were able to advance as far as the Tisza River, the limit proposed by the Paris Peace Conference. An armistice was agreed and the occupied area was then turned into a Romanian-controlled military district.

The Hungarian Red Army invaded the Czechoslovak state (the former Upper Hungary) in June 1919 instead and declared it a new Soviet Republic. Only then did the Hungarian patriots realise the communists were intent on spreading their form of politics as far as they could across Europe rather than just reclaiming their lost territories. Arguments over Hungary's future followed and the Hungarian Red Army fell apart as the nationalists and communists argued.

The Paris Peace Conference was still busy discussing Hungary's new borders, and while it was unhappy about the unauthorised advance into Hungary, Romania refused to withdraw its troops. The Peace Conference disapproved of the Hungarian advance into Czechoslovakia until the troops were withdrawn at the end of June.

Bucharest then turned its attention back to the Romanian occupation of its eastern territories. The Hungarian Red Army crossed the Tisza River on 20 July, hoping the Bolsheviks would attack Romania from the east. They did not and there had been no communist uprising by the time the Romanian counter-attack had driven the Hungarians back across the Tisza.

The Romanians entered Budapest on 3 August, bringing the short war between Hungary and Romania to an end. Kun went into exile in the Soviet Union while Gyula Peidl's new government faced a coup by the White House Fraternal Association. An attempt to make Archduke Joseph August of Austria, Hungary's head of state, with István Friedrich as his prime minister, failed.

The Treaty of Saint-Germain-en-Laye dealt with Austria in September 1919 and Romania signed a peace treaty with it. An Inter-Allied Military Mission supervised the disarming of Hungary, while Budapest was forced to pay reparations to Romania and for the cost of the occupation troops. However, Romania would not receive any reparation payments from Germany.

Most of the Romanian troops withdrew from Hungary early in 1920 and they took everything they could carry. A few units remained east of the Tisza River to maintain Bucharest's control. The Treaty of Trianon may have covered a peace agreement with Hungary in June 1920 but Budapest was still unhappy with the deal it had been forced to sign with Romania.

Bessarabia was another area Romania had coveted. The region had declared itself as the Moldavian Democratic Republic back in 1917 but the Romanian army had stepped in when the Bolsheviks threatened to take over. The area had declared its independence in January 1918 only to see the Bolsheviks interfere with its wish to become part of Romania. An attempt to form the Bessarabian Soviet Socialist Republic was stopped and while most of the region remained under Romanian rule, the area east of the River Dniester became the Moldavian Autonomous Soviet Socialist Republic in 1924.

Romania's huge growth addition in the aftermath of the Great War resulted in a self-belief which became known as 'Entire Romania'. It gave the Romanians greater confidence in a national identity enshrined in the new constitution, which was announced in 1923. However, regional identities and local culture suffered and the people living in the exchanged territories were soon opposed to the concept of a 'Greater Romania'.

King Ferdinand died in July 1927 but Prince Carol chose to renounce the throne and went into exile rather than give up an extra marital affair. It left his brother Nicolae as regent of Romania, until his young son Michael came of age. At the same time, Corneliu Codreanu formed the fascist Iron Guard; it was soon clashing with the long-established National Liberal Party (PNL) and Socialist Democratic Party (PSD), as well as the new National Peasant Party (PNT).

The Greco-Turkish War, 1919-22

The British, French and Italians had signed the St Jean-de-Maurienne Agreement, a plan to divide up Anatolia, in April 1917. British Prime Minister Lloyd George had also promised Greece extra territories if it joined the Allies' cause. The Ottoman Empire may have surrendered on 30 October 1918 but there were still many issues that needed to be resolved with Greece. Ethnic Greeks had been mistreated, deported and murdered since 1914, while a Relief Committee had been sending assistance to Anatolia since 1917. The abuse continued after the Armistice but the Entente was doing nothing to punish the perpetrators.

The Ottoman Empire faced being split into several states when Mustafa Kemal Atatürk started a nationalist revolution. The Entente supported the Greek plan to occupy Smyrna (now Izmir), a port on Anatolia's west coast, where 600,000 Orthodox Christians lived. Athens then intended to advance across Anatolia to protect the rest of the ethnic Greeks from persecution. Smyrna may have been promised to Italy but its poor performance in the war meant the pledge was revoked. The invasion of Anatolia was linked to Athens' ultimate goal, to retake Constantinople for Christendom. It could then recreate the ancient Greek empire which had once surrounded the Aegean Sea; a concept referred to as the Megali Idea.

The invasion started with British and French warships supporting the Greek navy as 20,000 soldiers were put ashore at Smyrna on 15 May 1919. The Turkish garrison surrendered and while the port's Christians saw the invasion force as liberators, the Muslims saw them as invaders. It would take twelve months to clear the Aegean coast, the first part of the Greek plan; it gave the Turks ample time to prepare for the second stage. They resisted the Greek advance towards the Büyük Menderes River (Meander), but most of western Anatolia was soon captured. The Allies rewarded Athens for its efforts under the Treaty of Sèvres, which was signed on 10 August 1920. Greece received eastern Thrace and the territorial rights to Smyrna while Turkey was forced to hand over the islands of Imbros and Tenedos. Control of the important Bosporus Straits, which gave access to the Black Sea, were placed under an International Commission. The Treaty may have resolved Russia's desire for access to the Mediterranean Sea but neither Greece nor the Ottoman Empire approved of the compromise decision.

The Treaty of Sèvres had divided the huge Ottoman Empire into several states while giving Britain, France and Italy areas to control. It also gave eastern Thrace and the area around Smyrna, on the west coast of Anatolia, to Greece. However, the Turkish government had refused to acknowledge the treaty, and the ethnic and religious massacres continued, culminating in what the Greeks called the 'Great Catastrophe'.

The Hellenic Army was starting the third part of its plan, an advance across Anatolia, in October 1920, when disaster struck in Athens. King Alexander died from an infection after he was bitten by a pet monkey. He left no heir, so Constantine was restored to the throne. A general election was due and while the royalists wanted to pursue the war in Anatolia, the republicans blamed the poor state of the economy on the invasion. The royalists lost the election on 1 November and Prime Minister Eleftherios Venizelos resigned and left the country.

King Constantine took the opportunity to put General Anastasios Papoulas in command of the Hellenic Army. He sacked any generals who opposed him and promoted loyal officers in their place; many others resigned in protest. All these changes were made while the Greeks advanced towards Ankara in the depths of winter.

Defeats at the First Battle of İnönü on 11 January 1921 and the Second Battle of İnönü on 27 March marked the beginning of the end for the Greek offensive. Britain dared not help in case they offended their allies, while France and Italy were busy selling supplies to the Turks. The Soviets were also supplying the Turkish revolutionaries under the Treaty of Moscow. Even so, the Hellenic Army reached the main railway in the summer, cutting Anatolia in two, forcing the Turks to withdraw east of the Sakarya. The Greeks might have followed them up but it would have left them in a vulnerable position.

A long stalemate over the winter was broken when French and Italian troops evacuated their positions. An Allied plea for armistice in March 1922 was refused by the Turkish leader Mustafa Kemal, because he was planning to counter-attack with Soviet weapons and supplies.

The Turks launched their Great Offensive at Dumlupınar in August 1922, driving the demoralised Greeks before them. They carried out a scorched earth policy as they fell back to the Aegean coast, while the Turks followed Mustafa Kemal's order: 'Your first goal is the Mediterranean, Forward!'

The Greek government resigned after Britain refused to arrange a truce. They had hoped the Hellenic Army could hold onto Smyrna, but Turkish troops entered the port on 9 September. Mustafa Kemal had insisted on a calm takeover, under the threat of death, but many atrocities were committed. Four days later the Greek and Armenian quarters of the city were set on fire and panic ensued as the population headed for the quayside. There was no means of escape; many burned to death, some drowned in the sea, others were murdered by the Turkish soldiers or their Muslim neighbours in the mayhem that followed. Estimates for the number of casualties range from 10,000 to 100,000. Around 200,000 left Smyrna for Greece, another 30,000 were deported across Asia Minor.

The final units of the Hellenic Army left the Aegean Coast on 18 September. They too had carried out many atrocities during the campaign, sometimes inspired by ethnic hatred and sometimes as revenge, after hearing about massacres of ethnic Greeks. As the Turkish army headed north to take control of the Bosporus Straits, the British wanted to stop them taking control of the Dardanelle Straits, to help the Greeks hold onto eastern Thrace. However, the French and Italian forces withdrew, leaving General Charles Harington no option but to persuade the Greek warships to leave Constantinople before any shots were fired. The British ground troops then convinced the Greek troops to withdraw behind the River Maritsa, to avoid armed confrontations in what was known as the Chanak Crisis. Only then would Mustafa Atatürk agree to hold armistice talks.

British, French and Italian troops occupied the disputed areas while the Hellenic Army withdrew under the Armistice of Mudros. The Turks claimed eastern Thrace, and while Britain wanted to hold onto Constantinople, the rest of the Allies refused to support it, to avoid another war. The Allies and the Turks eventually signed the Armistice of Mudanya in October 1922 and Britain decided to abandon eastern Thrace. Nine months later, the Treaty of Lausanne set a new border between Greece and Turkey, around

150 miles west of Constantinople. It meant that the access to the Black Sea was once again in Turkish hands.

The Treaty of Lausanne was signed in July 1923 and it brought to an end the ethnic violence. It also included an amnesty on the war crimes carried out by both sides to date. It is estimated that the Turkish regime had murdered around four million Armenians, Greeks, and Assyrians since 1900. The Greeks had also carried out many atrocities during their three-year campaign across Anatolia. To prevent further occurrences, the Greek and Turkish governments agreed to a population exchange to stop further occurrences. It resulted in 1.5 million Orthodox Christians being transferred from Turkey to Greece while half a million Muslims moved in the opposite direction.

The Second Hellenic Republic

Eleftherios Venizelos had taken control of Greece during World War I and he wanted to unite all the ethnic Greeks living around the Aegean Sea with a pro-republic, anti-communist country which supported the West. His style of politics was known as *Venizelism*.

The defeat of the Greek Army in the Asia Minor Campaign and its subsequent evacuation from Anatolia resulted in the resignation of Petros Protopapadakis's government in August 1922. Nikolaos Triantafyllakos took over as prime minister, only to face a republican coup on 11 September. A Revolutionary Committee sailed to Athens, forcing King Constantine I to go into exile, to make way for his son George II: the king would die soon afterwards. Sotirios Krokidas took control of the military government which marked the start of the Second Hellenic Republic. It also intensified the National Schism, as the country became entrenched into two points of view; the pro and the anti Venizelism supporters.

Greece declared it was a republic in March 1924 and the republicans won the referendum which followed. However, General Theodoros Pangalos seized control of the country in June 1925 and he immediately looked to seize territory from Bulgaria. A brief conflict ended when the League of Nations stepped in and the Greek troops withdrew behind their border. Athens was forced to pay Sofia compensation.

The expansion policies of Hitler led to Nazi Germany taking control of Austria and Czechoslovakia, north of Yugoslavia. Meanwhile, Mussolini's desire for Balkan territory led to Italian troops occupying Albania.

Chapter 4

Another War on the Horizon

November 1929 to September 1939

Alliances

A triple alliance replaced the Little Entente defence treaties between Yugoslavia, Czechoslovakia and Romania in June 1930 and it was recognised by the League of Nations. It would be replaced by a Pact of Organisation following Hitler's appointment as Chancellor of Germany in January 1933.

Mussolini was anxious to dominate Balkan politics so he could bully his way into seizing territory there. Bulgaria was also looking to reclaim the territories it had lost following the Great War. However, Yugoslavia, Romania, Greece and Turkey signed the Balkan Pact in February 1934 to counter Rome's and Sofia's plans. Greece had also befriended Britain because the Royal Navy had a large presence in the Eastern Mediterranean Sea, however London was anxious not to get involved in the Balkans.

Mussolini's answer to the Balkan Pact was to invade Abyssinia (now Ethiopia), in the horn of Africa, in October 1935. The conflict came after prolonged attempts to avert a crisis, which saw Italy leave the League of Nations (as Germany had done two years before). Mussolini wanted to imitate Hitler's desire to expand the Third Reich and did so by occupying Abyssinia in May 1936.

Timeline of the 1930s

June 1930	Yugoslavia, Czechoslovakia and Romania sign a triple alliance
May 1931	A right-wing coup takes control of Bulgaria
February 1933	Yugoslavia, Czechoslovakia and Romania sign the Pact of Organisation
February 1934	Yugoslavia, Romania, Greece and Turkey sign the Balkan Pact

October 1934   King Alexander of Yugoslavia is assassinated in Marseille, France

January 1935   Tsar Boris III takes back control of Bulgaria and runs it as a dictatorship

March 1937   Yugoslavia and Italy sign a friendship treaty

March 1938   The *Anschluss* (union between Nazi Germany and Austria)

October 1938   The Sudeten Crisis over Czechoslovakia

April 1939   Italian troops invade Albania

Yugoslavia in the 1930s

King Alexander increased his control over Yugoslavia by personally appointing members of parliament while banning secret ballots. Continuing Serb oppression of the Croats culminated with the arrest of the Croatian Peasant Party leader Vladko Maček, and the murder of the politician Milan Šufflay by police agents. King Alexander was looking to find a way to make the Serbs and Croats work together when he was murdered in Marseille on 9 October 1934. The assassination had been organised by the Croatian Ustaše and the Internal Macedonian Revolutionary Organization.

Alexander's son, Prince Peter II, was a minor, so a regency council took control of Yugoslavia on his behalf with the king's cousin, Prince Paul, as its main influencer. Ethnic tensions between the Serbs and the Croats intensified as they wrestled for control of the areas where they had a majority. They also both wanted to control the area where the Bosniak Muslims lived.

Josip Broz was released in March 1934 after five years in prison; he was determined to pursue his career in politics under the alias Tito. So he tracked down Milan Gorkić, the exiled leader of the Yugoslavian Communist Party, at his Vienna headquarters. He spent the next eighteen months working for the Communist International (Comintern) in the Soviet Union. He then returned to Yugoslavia to work for the Communist Party, only to hear that many of his colleagues in Moscow, including Gorkić, had been murdered. He left just before General Secretary of the Communist Party Joseph Stalin had launched the Great Purge (or Great Terror), which involved the execution of tens of thousands of politicians, government officials and army leaders, who were accused of spying or of being Trotskyists.

Tito was instructed to choose replacements for the murdered Yugoslav communists and to make sure that the Communist Party continued its work across Yugoslavia. He was promoted to secretary-general of the nation's party when he had completed the reorganisation.

Mussolini wanted to increase Italy's control of the Balkans, as the Nazis looked to unite the ethnic Germans across central Europe, and he planned to do it by stirring up trouble for Yugoslavia. Exiled Croatian nationalists continued to be welcomed in Italy, where Rome supported their Ustaše movement. Prince Paul eventually stopped this foreign interference in Yugoslavia's affairs by signing a friendship treaty with Mussolini in March 1937. Part of the deal involved arresting the leaders of the Ustaše and blocking the supply of money to the movement.

However, tensions across Europe soon overshadowed the problems across the Balkans, as the Nazis united ethnic Germans with their expansionist policies. Austria was first and the *Anschluss* with Germany brought the Third Reich to Yugoslavia's northern border in March 1938. Czechoslovakia was Hitler's next target, but Prince Paul refused to get involved in the Sudeten Crisis which reached a climax in October 1938. Germany would occupy the rest of Czechoslovakia over the next six months. Hitler then started threatening Poland.

Dragiša Cvetković, a Serb, was appointed prime minister of Yugoslavia, and Vladko Maček, a Croat, became vice premier in the summer of 1939. The compromise may have resulted in Croatia being allowed to hold its own parliament, but the hardline Ustaše still pursued full independence. The ongoing ethnic problems across Yugoslavia would make it vulnerable to interference from both Germany and Italy as Europe headed towards war.

Albania in the 1930s

Albania may have been on the long road to modernisation but the Wall Street Crash in the autumn of 1929 resulted in the nation having to extend its loans. A drought the following year required extra grain imports, increasing Albania's reliance on Italy and unable to repay the interest. It resulted in Rome demanding more concessions from Tirana. However, Zog forced the government to cut the nation's budget by 30 per cent rather than let Rome interfere in the running of the country. Albania also switched its trade from Italy to Yugoslavia and Greece. Mussolini retaliated by first halting the loan payments and then offered to increase them, as a bribe.

The austerity measures resulted in uprisings across Albania and Mussolini instructed the Italian Navy to deploy warships along the coast to increase the unrest. Zog was eventually forced to accept new loan repayments but there was worse to follow. He had also had to agree to allow Italian troops to take over key Albanian fortifications and Italian civilians to settle across the country. Many of them would be employed in the government ministries and the military. He had been forced to give Rome what it had always wanted: a say in the running of Albania, a vital stepping stone to taking over the country.

King Zog I refused to renew the Treaty of Tirana in 1931 but Italy would only allow Albania to trade with other countries with its approval. It put huge pressure on the nation's economy until the inevitable occurred in 1934: Tirana was unable to make its repayments. The plan had been for Italian warships to again deploy along the Albanian coast, creating a situation under which Italian troops could move in. However, the British Royal Navy intervened in the Adriatic Sea and Rome was forced to stand its armed forces down to avoid an armed confrontation.

Mussolini countered the alliance by invading Abyssinia (Ethiopia) in October 1935. It had come at the end of prolonged attempts to avert a crisis, in which Italy had left the League of Nations as Germany had done two years before. Mussolini wanted new territories and the occupation of Abyssinia in May 1936 imitated the expansion of the Third Reich.

Albania's economy improved with Italy's help after 1936, but so did Rome's influence over Tirana. Loans may have helped improve the country's industry and infrastructure but decisions were being manipulated by Italian civil servants. Rome also paid for the expansion to the Royal Albanian Army but again everything was under the direction of Italian military advisors.

The continued expansion of Nazi Germany irritated Mussolini, especially when Hitler failed to warn him about the occupation of the rump of Czechoslovakia in March 1939. He responded by ordering an invasion of Albania. After twenty years of trying to create a Balkan foothold by covert means, Mussolini was going to seize one by force. The fact that the Queen was due to give birth only served to hasten Mussolini's decision. He set the date for the invasion for 7 April 1939.

King Zog refused to hand over control of his kingdom in exchange for a huge bribe when the Italians issued their ultimatum on 25 March 1939. Then Prince Leka was born on 5 April and the Albanians took to the streets to celebrate the royal birth. They also protested against Rome's threats, as Italian aircraft flew low over their cities dropping propaganda leaflets. Two days later the *Regia Marina* (Italian navy) carried General Alfredo Guzzoni's 22,000-strong task force across the Adriatic Sea while 600 planes of the *Regia*

Aeronautica provided overhead cover. The Albanian people wanted to fight the invaders but the nation's small army was armed with outdated weapons. Italian troops seized control of key points in just a few days. Plans to fight on in the mountains were stopped by Italian agents who had been training the Albanian army.

King Zog and Queen Geraldine escaped across the border into Greece with their infant child. They would have to live out the rest of their lives in exile and it would be many years before Leka could return. They left behind a rioting mob who were powerless to stop the Italians seizing control of Albania. A few days later, Zog's old adversary Shefqet Vërlaci formed a fascist government which voted to unite Albania with Italy. King Zog was deposed in his absence while Italy's King Victor Emmanuel III was offered the crown; Francesco Jacomoni di San Savino was appointed the country's viceroy. The final act was for Albania to withdraw from the League of Nations; the takeover had taken just over a week.

The Italians then set about turning Albania into their own and thousands of colonists arrived to assist the puppet government run the state. Extra troops took over the military while militia legions were organised. Meanwhile, food and clothing were distributed across poor areas and political prisoners were released, going some way to appeasing the Albanians.

Romania in the 1930s

Carol returned to Romania in 1930. He promised to end his affair with Magda Lupescu, giving him the support of Iuliu Maniu and the National Peasants' Party. He was proclaimed king but it soon became clear that he had no desire to give up his mistress. It just gave the National Peasant Party and the Iron Guard another reason to challenge National Liberal Party's corrupt ways.

The Wall Street Crash of October 1929 had triggered a period of economic uncertainty and high unemployment in Romania. The King would often use his right under the 1923 constitution to dissolve parliament and call elections during this difficult period, resulting in a new government on average every six months.

The Iron Guard was banned in 1931, but Ion Duca went further in December 1933 by closing it down and arresting hundreds of members. The legionnaires would strike back just a few days later by assassinating the prime minister. The National Christian Defence League (*Liga Apărării*

Naţional Creştine or LANC) and the National Agrarian Party merged to form the National Christian Party (NCP) in the summer of 1935. The Iron Guard would rename itself 'Everything for the Fatherland' at the same time and Hitler told Carol that he wanted them to rule when they met.

Despite LANC's poor showing in the December 1937 election, King Carol decided to appoint its leader Octavian Goga prime minister. The government started implementing anti–Semitic policies, only for Goga to be dismissed just two months later for making derogatory remarks about the king's Jewish mistress. Carol decided to rule the country himself and his dictatorship was backed up by a new constitution.

The Iron Guard leader, Corneliu Codreanu, was arrested in April 1938 and it was announced that he and several of his comrades had died during an escape attempt in November 1938. In fact they had been murdered as revenge for several assassinations (Prime Minister Armand Călinescu would be assassinated by legionnaires avenging Codreanu's murder the following September).

Romania may have aligned with the Axis under Carol but both Great Britain and France were still anxious to keep Bucharest on their side. The two-stage occupation of Czechoslovakia in October 1938 and March 1939 prompted London and Paris to guarantee Romania's independence on 13 April 1939. Moscow refused to add their assurance to the guarantees.

Nazi Germany spent the summer putting pressure on Warsaw over its claims on the Polish Corridor, the area around Danzig which connected Pomerania and East Prussia. The Poles refused to hand the area over, angering Hitler. The world was then shocked when Germany and the Soviet Union signed a Treaty of Non-Aggression on 23 August 1939. It would have been even more shocked if they had known that the Foreign Ministers, Joachim von Ribbentrop and Vyacheslav Molotov, had also agreed a secret pact to divide Poland and the Baltic States between them. Bucharest would not have been surprised to learn that Moscow had an interest in Romania's north-east region, Bessarabia.

Britain and France signed an alliance with Poland only two days later but Hitler ignored it. The Luftwaffe started bombing targets across the country on 1 September while the Wehrmacht poured across the border. Warsaw decided against accepting military aid from Bucharest as Polish troops and civilians experienced the full terror of the German Blitzkrieg. Instead it relied on the promises from London and Paris to send aid via Romania's Black Sea ports.

Bulgaria in the 1930s

A coalition of the Democratic Alliance and the National Liberal Party had taken control of Bulgaria in January 1926. Prime Minister Andrey Lyapchev had obtained loans to boost the nation's economy but the Great Depression undermined the economy and a left-wing coalition won the 1931 elections. They faced opposition from the right-wing National Social Movement and the Military Union, who were soon plotting a coup. However, a society of army officers, called Link or *Zveno*, launched their own takeover bid on 19 May 1934 before Aleksandar Tsankov's National Social Movement could initiate theirs.

Kimon Georgiev took control and he closed down the National Assembly before abolishing the Tarnovo Constitution. The government also banned all opposition parties and replaced trade unions with state-run organisations. Tsar Boris III's role was downgraded to puppet but he soon started to plot a counter-coup with the assistance of loyal members of the Military Union. They would force Kimon Georgiev to resign in January 1935 and General Pencho Zlatev would act as Prime Minister until the country's situation stabilised.

Tsar Boris appointed Andrey Toshev as his prime minister but, being a mere puppet, was soon replaced by Georgi Kyoseivanov. The members of the Balkan Pact realised that Bulgaria was not a threat, so they asked it to sign the Salonica Pact in July 1938. Their united stance would counter Germany's aggressive stance towards the region.

Greece in the 1930s

The after effects of the 1929 Wall Street Crash undermined the Greek economy and Eleftherios Venizelos's government struggled to cope. General Ioannis Metaxas launched an anti-communist coup in March 1935, hoping to restore Greece's stability; but it failed. A second one, six months later, succeeded. General Georgios Kondylis abolished the republic and became both prime minister and regent, following a rigged referendum. King George II returned to Greece and was restored to the throne but the communists still held the balance of power, resulting in parliament having to be shut down. Metaxas eventually had to declare a state of emergency in August 1936 and then impose martial law to restore order following a general strike.

Metaxas ruled his new government as a dictatorship and adopted the title *Arhigos* or leader. The military restored order while the Secret Police or

Asfaleia identified enemies of the state. Political parties were closed down, strikes were banned and the media was censored. Around 15,000 suspected opponents of the regime were jailed or exiled to Aegean islands in the clampdown. Greek culture and nationalism were promoted while ethnic and religious minorities were persecuted. The National Organisation of Youth implemented a new curriculum which taught boys to prepare for the military, while girls learnt how to run a family home.

Greece may have had a totalitarian regime, but state control of industries proved popular because it improved working conditions. The nation did, however, face problems as political tensions across Europe increased as a result of Germany's expansion plans. The government may have been pro-German and King George may have been pro-British but Metaxas was anxious to keep Greece neutral.

An attempt to launch a coup in the port of Chania, on Crete, on 28 July 1938, failed. Troops were deployed to the island, and while some of the coup leaders escaped to Cyprus, the rest were deported. Metaxas responded by establishing a Provisional Military Court and declaring martial law across the country.

Greece wanted Britain's Royal Navy to counter the threat from Mussolini but London was wary about getting involved in Balkan politics. Metaxas even asked for an alliance with Britain following the Munich Conference (which handed the Sudetenland to Germany) in October 1938 but London still refused to get involved. Greece's need for support increased following Italy's invasion of Albania in April 1939 but it could not find any because all eyes were on central Europe, where Germany had just occupied Bohemia and Moravia.

The first Italian invasion failed over the winter of 1940/41. However, deployment of German troops in Bulgaria made sure that the second one in April 1941 was a success. The mainland fell quickly and then an airborne attack captured the island of Crete.

Chapter 5

The Invasion of Greece

October 1940 to April 1941

The Italian Desire for Living Space

Mussolini had been yearning for living space, or *spazio vitale*, for Italy's increasing population since the late 1920s. His plan had been initially to take control of Albania and Dalmatia, Yugoslavia's coastal territory. Italy could then expand its influence across the rest of Yugoslavia and into Greece to increase its hold on the Balkans. However, Mussolini started looking elsewhere in the 1930s, either to draw attention from domestic problems or to increase control over the Red Sea and the Middle East. Italian troops instead attacked Abyssinia (now Ethiopia) from Italian East Africa in October 1935. Mussolini then sent troops and supplies to Spain where they supported General Francisco Franco's nationalist victory.

Mussolini announced that Greece was a threat to Italy's expansion plans in February 1939, while his response to Hitler completing the occupation of Czechoslovakia was to order an invasion of Albania in April. Tirana would surrender after only a few days, leaving Athens wondering when its turn would come.

Mussolini followed Nazi Germany's invasion of France by declaring war on France and Great Britain in June 1940. However, the Italian troops had little to do because France surrendered to Germany a few days later, while the British Army was evacuated from Dunkirk.

Relations between Greece and Italy had continued to deteriorate, due to anti-Greek propaganda in the Italian media and incidents along the border between Albania and Greece. However, Ioannis Metaxas kept Greece neutral, even after an Italian submarine torpedoed and sank the cruiser *Elli* on 15 August 1940. Britain had guaranteed Greece's independence, but all London could do was deploy Royal Navy warships to the Eastern Mediterranean as a threat. In return, Athens agreed that Greek merchant ships would help the British war effort in North Africa. Rome considered the convoys to be legitimate targets and they were often subjected to air attacks or stalked by submarines.

Hitler was against further Italian involvement in the Balkans for the time being and he asked Mussolini to focus on knocking Britain out of the war. That involved invading Egypt with a view to cutting the Suez Canal, the British Empire's route for its oil and other supplies. Operation E began in September 1940 but the Italian troops only advanced a short distance before they stopped to build supply camps ready for the final advance. The British counterattack, codenamed Operation Compass, captured nearly 140,000 prisoners and hundreds of tanks, aircraft and artillery pieces in December. It left a furious Mussolini having to cancel his plans to seize Yugoslavia.

Meanwhile, there were developments in Romania, which had just been taken over by the fascist group called the Iron Guard. Hitler was anxious to secure the Ploieşti oil fields, north of Bucharest, and he offered to send German troops to protect them. They started crossing the border on 7 October and half a million were soon deployed across the country. Another Axis ally had been secured but Mussolini was again angry that Hitler had failed to tell him. He retaliated by planning to expand his foothold in the Balkans, and that meant using Albania as a base from which to invade Greece.

The build-up to War

Mussolini's plan was to split the Adriatic coastal regions of Epirus and Acarnania from the rest of Greece. Italy could then take control of the Ionian Islands in the Adriatic Sea and the Dodecanese Islands in the Aegean Sea; he would install a puppet regime to run the rest of mainland Greece.

Unfortunately, reforms recently implemented by the Chief of Staff, Marshal Pietro Badoglio, had left Italy's armed forces with many problems. Not least that around 900,000 regular and reservist soldiers had to be allowed home to collect the autumn harvest. Bureaucracy and politics only served to increase the inefficiency, leaving many units armed with obsolete weapons, while a shortage of lorries left the army reliant on horse-drawn transport.

Mussolini had wanted Bulgaria to make a simultaneous attack against north-east Greece, starting on 26 October, but Tsar Boris III refused to cooperate because it was a member of the Balkan Pact. It meant the Italian units advancing through western Macedonia would have an exposed flank. General Mario Roatta argued that he needed more troops to capture Epirus, under the plan codenamed 'Contingency G'. However, General Sebastiano Visconti Prasca convinced Mussolini otherwise, so the attack would go ahead as planned.

Greece had never seen Albania or Yugoslavia as a threat throughout the 1930s, and Athens had always focused on protecting itself from Bulgaria. So the armed forces had invested a huge amount of resources in a series of forts across Eastern Macedonia and the Western Thrace border, called the Metaxas Line. However, the Italian invasion of Albania in April 1939 meant Greece's armed forces had to plan how to guard against a coordinated attack by Italy and Bulgaria instead. Plan IB was then revised to Plan IBa following the German invasion of Poland on 1 September, but Athens was still convinced Bulgaria was the biggest threat. It meant money continued to be lavished on the Metaxas Line.

The Greek army had insufficient troops to hold its 400-mile-long northern border. It could only spare a single division to hold the Epirus region facing Albania, while another four, grouped under the Western Macedonia Army Section, faced the Yugoslav frontier. The rest of the Greek divisions were stretched along the Metaxas Line. The 1935 Balkan Pact ensured that the Bulgarians would not attack, so General Alexandros Papagos had been able to distribute his troops more evenly along the border.

The Royal Hellenic Air Force would find itself equipped with too few out-of-date planes by the end of the 1930s. Several British Royal Air Force squadrons had been sent from Egypt to support them but they would make little difference. The Royal Hellenic Navy had an inadequate mixture of old and new warships, submarines and torpedo boats to patrol its coastal waters.

The Italian Invasion of Greece, October 1940 to March 1941

The Italian army faced a difficult advance on a narrow front, with few roads for the armour and even fewer opportunities to make outflanking manoeuvres. The Pindus Mountains divided the front into two, and XXVI Corizza Corps would advance inland through Western Macedonia while XXV Ciamuria Corps followed the Adriatic Coast. Roatta asked for more time to complete his deployment. He was given just two days, but it was enough for the Greeks to transfer reinforcements from the Bulgarian to the Epirus front.

Italy's ambassador in Athens, Emanuele Grazzi, issued an ultimatum for free passage for Italian troops late on 28 October 1940. Ioannis Metaxas refused to bow to the demand and the invasion began shortly afterwards. Greece still celebrates the day, calling it their 'No Anniversary'.

XXVI Corizza Corps advanced first and it initially made good progress around Konista, but poor weather stalled the advance after only a few days. The Italians were left stranded in the Pindus Mountains and Greek reinforcements overran the Julia Division. The rest of XXVI Corps was forced to withdraw towards the Albanian border.

XXV Ciamuria Corps' attack into Epirus had started on 2 November but little progress was made towards Ioannina. The advance down the coast towards Preveza did no better because of the lack of good roads. Meanwhile, bad weather had prevented an amphibious landing on Corfu. The heroic defence of the border area would be remembered as a triumph across Greece and referred to as the 'Epic of 1940'.

Mussolini sacked General Sebastiano Prasca and sent his State Under-secretary of War, Ubaldo Soddu, to the front line to resume the offensive. However, he soon discovered that the Italian troops were short of everything because supplies were having to be shipped across the Adriatic to the ports of Valona and Durrës. He also learnt that the Italians were outnumbered by as much as two-to-one in places and so he asked for reinforcements as his men dug in.

Unfortunately for the Italians, they focused on holding the valleys while the Greeks advanced though the Morava and the Ivan Mountains, starting on 14 November. They secured the Korçë plateau and headed towards the port of Valona, threatening to cut the Italian supply line. Mussolini replaced Badoglio with General Ugo Cavallero but he too was unable to stop the Greek troops advancing into Albania.

The Italians were less than eager about launching a second attack against Greece, after its failure over the winter of 1940-41. They became even less enthusiastic following the catastrophic outcome of the British advance across North Africa, which started in December 1940. Operation Compass resulted in 138,000 Italian soldiers and hundreds of tanks, guns and aircraft being taken prisoner. An angry Mussolini responded by ordering all senior members of the National Fascist Party to the front line.

The winter weather had made it difficult to keep the front line supplied and the Greeks had captured more areas from the Italians, including the Trebeshinë Mountains, by January 1941. This time it was the Greeks who ran short of supplies and they had to go over to the defensive. Their generals were sacked as they argued over strategy.

The Ultra codebreakers based in Britain had often intercepted Italian Air Force messages, allowing them to guide Royal Air Force fighter squadrons to intercept the bombers. They had become so skilled at breaking the codes that they were disrupting most of the Italian air operations by the spring of 1941. Meanwhile, the RAF bomber squadrons had done what they could to support the Greeks, in spite of the winter weather.

Operation Marita, the Axis Invasion of Greece, April 1941

Great Britain may have deployed troops to secure its bases on the islands of Crete and Lemnos, but Hitler still wanted to capture them so the German navy and air force could interdict Allied shipping lanes across the Mediterranean Sea. A plan for the invasion of Greece from Bulgaria, codenamed Operation Marita, had been issued on 13 December 1940.

Alexandros Koryzis became prime minister of Greece after Metaxas died in January 1941 but King George continued to control the country. Prime Minister Winston Churchill decided he wanted to fight in the Balkans, but Britain was limited in what could be sent because of its commitment to the North African campaign. General Alexandros Papagos initially refused to accept what was offered, believing it would give the Germans an excuse to attack.

Lieutenant General Sir Henry Maitland Wilson had eventually organised W Force in Egypt by February 1941. Nearly 60,000 troops were shipped to Piraeus, near Athens, under the codename Operation Lustre, starting on 4 March. The Italian Fleet intended to attack the convoys, only the Ultra codebreakers told the Mediterranean Fleet when they were approaching. It meant the Royal Navy were able to sink five warships at the Battle of Cape Matapan on 28 March.

The British and Empire troops may have deployed on the northern border in time but they were more than matched by the movement of German troops into Bulgaria and the mobilisation of the Bulgarian Army. The Italians had also reinforced their front when the weather allowed, with a view to driving the Greeks back across the Albanian border before the Germans became involved. The advance towards Ioannina on 9 March was soon stopped, but it left the Greeks short of ammunition. Prime Minister Alexandros Koryzis did ask the British for supplies, but it would take time to deliver them and the Greek army did not have time.

The problem was that Operation Marita would be brought forward following a coup d'état in Yugoslavia on 27 March. Hitler ordered a combined attack by German and Italian forces, supported by Bulgarian and Hungarian troops, against both Greece and Yugoslavia on 6 April.

The situation may have stabilised along the Albanian front but the covert movement of thousands of German troops into Bulgaria changed the balance of power. They deployed, poised to invade Eastern Macedonia and Western Thrace, where the Eastern Macedonia Army Section only had 70,000 men stretched out along the Metaxas Line. The Central Macedonia Army Section was even more vulnerable, since German troops were deploying opposite the sector.

The Allied Deployment

General Alexandros Papagos faced difficult decisions over how to defend Greece's long border. Most of his troops were engaged in Albania, leaving only 70,000 men to hold the Metaxas Line. The British and Empire troops of W Force had deployed in the western Macedonian mountains. The 6th Australian Division held the Haliacmon valley and the Vermion Mountains, while the 2nd New Zealand division dug in north of Mount Olympus. The 1st British Armoured Brigade was supposed to give support but the narrow mountain roads would make it difficult to deploy.

W Force was holding a weak position because all the supplies had to be delivered across the Mediterranean Sea to Thessaloniki, and the port was only fifty miles from the Bulgarian border. The Germans could easily capture Thessaloniki, cutting General Wilson's supply route. The Wehrmacht's armoured columns could then drive south along the Aegean coast towards Athens while the Luftwaffe would bomb the port of Pireas/ Piraeus to stop the British and Empire troops escaping. General Wilson's request to withdraw from the extended front had been overruled by the Greeks.

The German Invasion

The Yugoslav coup d'état on 27 March 1941 required the Axis to make a late change in plan, involving a simultaneous attack against Yugoslavia and Greece on 6 April. Field Marshal Wilhelm List's Twelfth Army advanced across the Bulgarian-Greek border in two columns as the Luftwaffe rained bombs down on the Greek cities and ports.

The western armoured column had soon reached Prilep, cutting the rail connection between Yugoslavia and Greece. It then headed south through Monastir (now Bitola) and Florina, before turning west to meet the Italians along the Albanian border. The eastern column advanced south through Strumica, capturing the port of Thessaloniki after only three days. In doing so, they had cut off the Eastern Macedonia Army Section in the Metaxas Line. General Wilson's concerns had come true.

The Greek-Yugoslav Counter Offensive

The Allies planned to counter the German attack by driving the Italians out of Albania, and the Western Macedonia Army Section advanced along the Adriatic coast towards Durrës on 7 April. The Third Yugoslav Army crossed the River Drin at the same time but its advance was compromised by the loss of Skopje. A counter-attack by German and Italian units then forced the Yugoslavs to retreat and they took over 30,000 prisoners.

The Metaxas Line

Lieutenant General Konstantinos Bakopoulos had far too few men to man the Metaxas Line effectively. The first attack on 6 April was stopped, so German armoured columns withdrew to let the artillery and air force bomb and shell the forts into submission. Meanwhile, mountain troops found an unguarded pass through the Rodopi Mountains and crossed the River Struma. The railway to Thessaloniki was cut and its harbour captured, forcing Bakopoulos to surrender on 9 April. It had taken only seventy-two hours to capture Western Thrace.

Twelfth Army forced its way through the Monastir Gap and headed south to reach Kozani, while Australian and New Zealand troops fought a series of rearguard actions. Field Marshal Wilhelm List's armour may have been stopped for the time being but the Luftwaffe continued to bomb Volos port to the south. Wilson had been left with no option but to abandon Mount Olympus and withdraw his troops through Thermopylae so they could be evacuated from Volos harbour. The German tanks struggled to negotiate the mountain roads, enabling the 2nd New Zealand Division and 6th Australian Division to hold on for a week before withdrawing to Thebes.

The Epirus Army Section may have fought on in Albania but the Twelfth German Army was able to advance through Western Macedonia before swinging behind its rear. First Grevena and then Ioannina fell, cutting off the Greek Epirus Army. The order to withdraw from the Albanian front was issued on 12 April but it came too late to save the Greeks. They had reached the end of their endurance after fighting for five months, so General Ioannis Pitsikas asked General Alexandros Papagos if he could surrender to the Germans rather than to the Italians. Pitsikas then refused to negotiate with the Germans, so General Georgios Tsolakoglou was appointed to carry out the odious task. Tsolakoglou and *Obergruppenführer* Sepp Dietrich signed the surrender document on 20 April. Pitsikas resigned in disgust.

The surrender compromised Wilson's position because the Germans were able to capture the main British supply depot at Larissa airfield. Their tanks would reach Volos port on 21 April, just after the last Allied ship had left. The capitulation had denied the Italians the victory they desired after six months of fighting and an angry Mussolini made sure he was represented during the signing of the armistice on 23 April. He was even further irritated by the fact that the Greek troops were allowed home after demobilisation.

German motorised troops either fought or bypassed the British rear-guards as they fell back towards Athens; they entered the capital on 27 April. They drove straight to the Acropolis, the iconic ancient citadel overlooking the city, and raised the Nazi flag. Legend tells us that Konstantinos Koukidis, a member of the Greek presidential guard known as the *Evzone*, lowered the Greek flag, wrapped it around his body and jumped to his death.

The Evacuation of Mainland Greece

General Wilson and General Archibald Wavell (the commander of British Army forces in the Middle East) had discussed how W Force could be withdrawn. However, they did not speak to the Greeks about the eventuality until General Alexandros Papagos suggested it was wise to organise an evacuation. A despondent Prime Minister Alexandros Koryzis committed suicide on hearing the news.

Rear Admiral Harold Baillie-Grohman travelled to Greece to arrange the evacuation and the plan was to send part of W Force to Egypt while the rest reinforced the garrison defending the island of Crete. The Luftwaffe were targeting Pireas, Athens's main port, so the Empire troops had to head to smaller harbours and then wait to be evacuated at night. Ships took the New Zealanders from Porto Rafti harbour, east of Athens, late on 24 April, while the Australians were evacuated from Megara and Nafplio, south-west of the capital, the following night. Navigating in the darkness was dangerous and several hundred Australians had to spend an additional two nights onboard after their ship ran aground.

Greek ships had been directed to evacuate the Allied troops to Crete, while rearguards held the Corinth Canal. However, German glider troops crossed the canal on 25 April, leaving the Allies looking for other ways to reach the coast. The air raids continued and over twenty-five troop ships would be sunk, resulting in hundreds of deaths. German armour reached the south coast on 29 April and while over 40,000 troops had been evacuated, around 8,000, many of them Australian, had been left behind.

Operation Mercury, The Battle of Crete, May 1941

British and Empire troops had deployed to Crete when the Italians invaded Greece in October 1940. It was an important location in the eastern Mediterranean Sea because it had harbours for the Royal Navy and airfields for the Royal Air Force. Royal Navy and Greek ships may have evacuated 57,000 British, Commonwealth and Greek troops to Egypt and Crete but they had been forced to leave all their heavy equipment behind.

The Wehrmacht had to turn its attentions to the imminent invasion of the Soviet Union, codenamed Operation Barbarossa, but the Luftwaffe believed it could launch an airborne attack to capture Crete. Hitler agreed, believing that the island's harbours and airfields could be used to dominate the Eastern Mediterranean.

The build-up to the Battle

Hitler issued orders to the Luftwaffe to launch its largest airborne invasion of the war on 25 April. It would be codenamed Operation Mercury. Fliegerkorps VIII had 430 bombers and 180 fighters ready to knock out the airfields and anti-aircraft units stationed across Crete. Meanwhile, Fliegerkorps XI assembled its transport planes and gliders as soon as enough airfields had been built around Athens. The plan was for 7th Flieger Division to drop the paratroopers onto the airfields so the gliders could deliver heavy weapons and supplies to them. The 5th Mountain Division would then land, ready to attack other objectives across the island.

New Zealand Army officer Major General Bernard Freyberg VC was appointed commander of Crete on 30 April 1941. He took control of the 14,000-strong garrison but had little time to organise the 25,000 British and Empire troops who had just arrived from mainland Greece. Many had no weapons and the Luftwaffe were attacking the supply ships, so they could neither be evacuated nor armed. Freyberg had planned to block the airfields' runways but Middle East Command ordered him to keep them open for the Royal Air Force. It would prove to be a fatal decision.

Freyberg's main advantage was that the British code breakers had been tracking Fliegerkorps XI's deployment across the Balkans and learned that its target was Crete on 26 April. The information was confirmed on 1 May when the Luftwaffe stopped bombing and started photographing the island's airfields.

Major General Kurt von Student had to improvise plans for Operation Mercury because of the short notice he had been given and he divided his force into three *Kampfgruppen* or battlegroups. *Generalmajor* Eugen Meindl's *Kampfgruppe* COMET had to capture Maleme airfield at the west end of the island so that heavy weapons could be landed. *Generalmajor* Wilhelm Süssmann's *Kampfgruppe* Mars had to secure the coastal area around Souda Bay so the ships could land reinforcements. Only then could *Oberst* Bruno Bräuer's *Kampfgruppe* Orion attack the capital, Heraklion, in the centre of the island.

Student's plan was for around 530 Ju52 transport aircraft to drop 10,000 paratroopers around the Cretan airfields. Once they were secure, 100 gliders could land 5,000 mountain troops and heavy weapons on the runways. The German and Italian navies were on standby to deliver 7,000 troops. It may have seemed like a large force but the German intelligence service, the *Abwehr*, had seriously underestimated the number of Allied troops on the island. It had also misjudged the Cretan reception to the invasion, believing that the locals would welcome the 'liberation' of their island.

Paratroopers landed around Maleme airfield and Chania on the morning of 20 May 1941 but the New Zealand troops inflicted heavy casualties. It would leave the glider troops having to fend for themselves when they landed. Some of the paratroopers and gliders landed in the wrong place and it was some time before they were ready to attack. The second wave of troops secured Rethymno in the afternoon but those who landed around Heraklion faced heavy resistance from British, Australian and Greek troops.

The New Zealanders accidently abandoned Hill 107 late on 20 May, compromising the defences around Maleme. It was just one of the many misunderstandings caused by poor communications and confusion which handed control of the airfield to the Germans. The Allied troops then had to face the threat of German reinforcements landing near Maleme, until the convoy was intercepted by Naval Task Force D. Around 300 German troops were drowned and while only 100 reached the coast safely, they had diverted reinforcements from the airfield. Dive bombers then hit the Allied positions around Heraklion while the paratroopers took control of Maleme airfield.

Transport planes ferried 5th Mountain Division to Crete during the night, reinforcing the airfield area. The New Zealand counter-attack was delayed until the early hours of 22 May and air attacks at dawn forced them to withdraw. Naval Task Force C hunted down a second German flotilla on 23 May, and while it had no ammunition to engage the transports, it did force them to abort their landing. Force C then rendezvoused with Force A1, only to lose two cruisers and a destroyer to further Luftwaffe attacks. The 5th Destroyer Flotilla from Malta was able to rescue the survivors before the Luftwaffe found them and then turned its guns on the Germans around Maleme.

Meanwhile, the Allies were preparing to head into the mountains with a view to being evacuated by the Royal Navy, but they would have to fight their way out. New Zealand and Australian troops first had to clear German troops from the road between Souda and Chania, in what became known as the Battle of 42nd Street. Around 800 commandos of Layforce, who had recently landed at Souda Bay, then formed rearguards, so the tired Crete garrison could escape. But not everyone got away; some like the New Zealanders and Greeks holding Kissamos, on the west coast, were overrun.

The German paratroopers and mountain troops were starting to tire, so 3,000 Italian troops were landed around Sitia, at the east end of the island. They advanced towards the Germans at Ierapetra on the south coast, finding the Allies had already left. Wavell reported to Winston Churchill that the island could not be held any longer, so the race was on to evacuate as many Allied troops as possible.

The evacuation of troops to Egypt began late on 28 May while German fighters and bombers attacked the ships at every opportunity. Around 9,500 men were taken from Heraklion and 6,000 troops were rescued from the tiny harbours along the Sfakia coast late on 29 May; another 3,000 were evacuated from other harbours. The Germans linked up with the Italian troops who had landed at Sitia on 30 May and Colonel Ian Campbell surrendered Heraklion the following day. Another 5,000 waiting to be evacuated from Sfakia also surrendered.

Operation Mercury had taken an important objective in just a few days. It had caused nearly 3,500 Allied casualties on land and another 2,000 at sea; another 20,000 had been taken prisoner. However, the German victory had come at a cost. There had been over 6,500 casualties, while nearly 300 planes had been destroyed or damaged. It led to the end of German airborne operations; the paratroopers would fight on the ground in future.

Many Cretans had opposed the Germans with any weapon that came to hand, rather than welcoming them as the Germans had expected. It resulted in hundreds of locals being executed, both during the battle and afterwards, including nearly 200 at the village of Alikianos and a similar number at Kondomari. Some Cretans continued to fight the occupying forces long after the last Allied ship had left, alongside the 500 Allied troops who had refused to surrender. Their activities resulted in more massacres and the demolition of many villages.

The Cost of the Greek Campaign

The Axis may have had control of the Eastern Mediterranean Sea but it had come at a high cost and taken longer than expected. The Italians had started the campaign back in October 1940, with just 87,000 troops advancing from Albania. Mussolini had been forced to ask Hitler for help when they had been driven back. Eventually over 560,000 Italian troops had to be deployed to the Balkans and they had to be supported by 450 planes and 160 tanks. Over 100,000 would become casualties, most during the first campaign.

Germany had to deploy another 680,000 troops to the Balkans and they were backed up by around 1,200 tanks and 700 aircraft. The overwhelming support meant that only 5,200 casualties fell during the battle for mainland Greece. More were suffered during the airborne attack on Crete.

The Greeks may have had 420,00 soldiers deployed to defend their country but they were only supported by twenty tanks. Over 57,000 were killed or wounded and another 270,000 were taken prisoner. Over 60,000 British, Australian and New Zealand troops had been sent to help the Greeks, but they too were overwhelmed by the Axis onslaught. Over 2,100 were killed or wounded and 14,000 captured on the mainland. Another 6,000 casualties were suffered during the battle for Crete and over 17,500 taken prisoner.

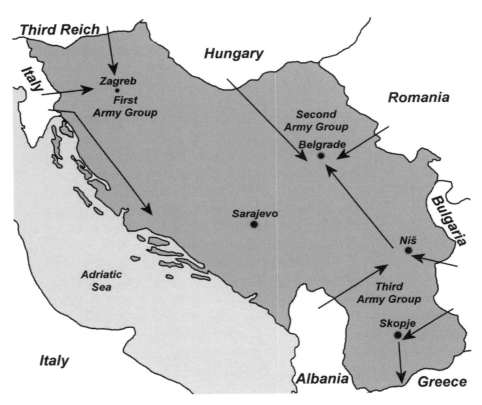

The combined armed forces of Germany and Italy crushed Yugoslav resistance in a matter of days. Romanian and Hungarian troops then moved in to occupy parts of the country.

Chapter 6

The Invasion of Yugoslavia

April 1941

Surrounding Yugoslavia

Nazi Germany had shared a border with Yugoslavia since the Anschluss with Austria in March 1938. Italy had shared a border with it since invading Albania twelve months later. Hungary and then Romania joined the Axis, leaving Yugoslavia virtually surrounded by the members of the Tripartite Pact.

One reason behind Hitler's desire to invade Yugoslavia went back to Italy's failed invasion of Greece in October 1940. German units had to be sent to help Mussolini's troops hold their positions in Albania. However, the main reason for taking control of the Balkans was oil; Romania was contributing nearly half of Germany's supply. Hitler was planning to invade the Soviet Union and he wanted to make sure Britain's Royal Air Force could not bomb the Ploieşti oilfields. That meant the Axis had to have control of Greece and Yugoslavia.

Hitler offered Hungary territory along its border with Yugoslavia in return for its support and it joined the Tripartite Pact in November 1940. Prime Minister Pál Teleki was against allowing German troops to pass through Hungary en route to the Romanian oilfields, but he was overruled. It left only Yugoslavia to sign the Tripartite Pact and Budapest signed a non-aggression pact with Belgrade on 12 December to pave the way. Teleki would commit suicide when the Wehrmacht crossed the Hungarian border in April 1941, only days before the invasion of Yugoslavia and Greece.

King Carol II had declared Romanian neutrality when Germany invaded Poland on 1 September 1939. He then allowed 120,000 Polish troops to withdraw through his country following the Soviet invasion on 17 September so they could fight again in France. Legionnaires of the Iron Guard struck back by assassinating Prime Minister Armand Călinescu a few days later, both with the approval and the assistance of Berlin.

Carol had promised a defensive line would protect Romania from attack but nothing was done to build one. He managed to stay neutral over the winter even though the British Expeditionary Force had evacuated from Dunkirk to Britain in May 1940 and France had surrendered a month later. During the summer the Axis punished Romania by confiscating the territories awarded to it after the First World War. Parts of the north-east regions of Bessarabia and Bukovina were ceded to the Soviets. Then northern Transylvania was given to Hungary under the Second Vienna Award. Finally, part of the southern region of Dobruja was handed to Bulgaria under the Treaty of Craiova.

Opposition to King Carol's neutral stance grew, and Ion Gigurtu had formed a new government which included Iron Guard leader Horia Sima, an established fascist and anti-Semite. General Ion Antonescu then joined forces with the Iron Guard and they declared a new National Legionary State; an authoritarian state. Antonescu was named *Conducător*, with Sima as his deputy.

King Carol was forced to abdicate in September 1940 and he headed into exile with his mistress Magda Lupescu. His 19-year-old son, Prince Michael, was returned to the throne as the Wehrmacht crossed the Romanian border to protect the Ploieşti oil refineries. Antonescu withdrew Romania from the Balkan Pact at the end of September and he instead joined the Tripartite Pact and the Anti-Comintern Pact at the end of November. Romania would eventually join the Axis powers at the end of November 1940 and the new regime was heralded with rallies and an increase of anti-Semitic legislation. The Iron Guard's dead leader, Corneliu Codreanu, was reburied in a huge ceremony, while over sixty political opponents were executed in Jilava prison. The takeover was also marked by the forced relocation of 75,000 ethnic Germans to Germany; their place was taken by Romanian refugees sent from Bulgaria.

Germany could then deploy troops across Romania under the excuse that they were going to train the armed forces. Great Britain would eventually cut diplomatic ties on the grounds that it was becoming an occupied country. Differences between Antonescu and Sima would lead to a coup by the Iron Guard on 20 January 1941. The armed forces stopped them and many legionnaires escaped into Germany, while their comrades were imprisoned; nearly 2,000 would be executed. Antonescu then announced Romania was going to become a National and Social State.

Antonescu learnt that Hitler intended to launch an attack on the Soviet Union in the spring of 1941 and Romania would be the jumping-off point for

Army Group South's advance into the Ukrainian Soviet Socialist Republic. However, the Führer wanted to secure the Balkans first and that involved occupying Yugoslavia and Greece. The Italians had failed to capture Greece when they attacked in October 1940. The deployment of 500,000 German troops across Romania over the winter meant that a combined attack had a much greater chance of success.

Rumours that the British Royal Air Force was planning to bomb the Romania oilfields prompted Hitler to discuss how to defend Bulgarian airspace with Tsar Boris III. The Luftwaffe had moved large numbers of planes into Bulgaria by the time it joined the Tripartite Pact on 1 March 1940; the Wehrmacht crossed the border the following day.

Closing in on Yugoslavia

Hungary and Romania were already members of the Axis Tripartite Pact and Hitler was pressurising Yugoslavia to join as well. Yugoslavia's Prime Minister Dragiša Cvetković and Foreign Minister Aleksandar Cincar-Marković visited Hitler on 14 February 1941 to discuss joining, but Bulgaria would join first. German troops were moving into it as the Yugoslav regent, Prince Paul, spoke to the Führer on 4 March 1941. Germany was planning to invade the Soviet Union and Hitler was anxious to secure the Balkans and the Romanian oilfields against attacks from the British and Empire troops who had recently reinforced the Greek army.

Prince Paul eventually signed on 25 March 1941, only to see the military seize control of his country just two days later. Paul was immediately replaced by his 17-year-old nephew, who was declared King Peter II despite his young age. A furious Hitler wanted 'to destroy Yugoslavia militarily and as a state with pitiless harshness and without waiting for possible declarations of loyalty of the new government'.

The German embassy in Belgrade was evacuated on 2 April and plans were issued the following day; Yugoslavia would be invaded on 6 April. Operation 25 would include attacks from Hungary, Romania, and Bulgaria, where the Wehrmacht and Luftwaffe had already deployed along the border under different cover stories.

Yugoslav Coup d'État, 27 March 1941

Prince Paul had been trying to strengthen his country's weak position by negotiating with the leading Croat politician Vladko Maček. Meanwhile,

Prime Minister Milan Stojadinović assured Hitler that Yugoslavia would not interfere in the Anschluss between Germany and Austria in March 1938. It left the Third Reich as Yugoslavia's neighbour.

Voting rules meant that Maček's United Opposition only got 20 per cent of the seats in the National Assembly despite receiving 45 per cent of the votes in the December 1938 election. It was clear that the Serbs would always dominate Yugoslav politics while the Serbian paramilitary Green Shirt group made Stojadinović look more like a fascist dictator.

Prince Paul eventually replaced Stojadinović with Dragiša Cvetković, and he was told to work with Maček to bring the Serbs and Croats closer together. They eventually agreed that there would be a province (*banovina*) of Croatia. Attentions then turned to Poland in September 1939, when first Nazi Germany and then the Soviet Union invaded it.

British intelligence agencies were working to keep Yugoslavia neutral but attention switched to Greece in October 1940 when Italian troops attacked. The Greeks stopped the invasion but there were concerns that Germany would want to help its ally. Both Hungary and Romania had joined the Tripartite Pact by November 1940 and General Milan Nedić suggested Yugoslavia should join as well. Prince Paul disagreed and he replaced Nedić with General Petar Pešić. A non-aggression pact with Hungary did little to alleviate Yugoslavia's troubles while Britain ignored Belgrade's requests for military aid.

Hitler asked Prime Minister Dragiša Cvetković to demobilise the Yugoslav armed forces and to join the Tripartite Pact but he refused. The Balkan situation then took a turn for the worse in February 1941 after Bulgaria and Turkey signed a friendship agreement. Bulgaria then signed the Tripartite Pact on 1 March, allowing German troops to deploy along the Yugoslav border.

Prince Paul offered Hitler a non-aggression pact and a declaration of friendship when they met on 4 March but the Führer wanted Yugoslavia to join the Tripartite Pact. Belgrade then secretly asked Moscow for an alliance, only to be told the Soviet Union was honouring the Molotov-Ribbentrop Pact of non-belligerence, which had been signed with Germany in August 1939. Hitler gave Prince Paul a final chance to join the Tripartite Pact and he signed on 25 March.

General Dušan Simović's group of Army Air Force officers had been talking about a coup for some time, because they were both anti-Axis and pro-Serb. The signing of the pact meant they had to act immediately and members of the British Special Operations Executive (SOE) encouraged the plan. Two days later, the Yugoslav Army Air Force deputy commander, Borivoje Mirković, deployed troops and tanks across the country. At the same time, Deputy Prime Minister Maček took Prince Paul to meet the army commander August Marić and the Croatian politician Ivan Šubašić. Paul decided not to oppose the coup and instead headed to Belgrade, where he abdicated before heading into exile with his family.

Seventeen-year-old King Peter II was declared old enough to take the throne in his place, while Yugoslav troops surrounded the palace. Planes dropped propaganda leaflets, while a spokesman impersonating Prince Paul made a radio broadcast, telling the people to support Peter. Tens of thousands responded by demonstrating on the streets under slogans such as 'Better the war than the pact' and 'Better the grave than a slave'. King Peter II was inaugurated on 28 March, bringing to an end a peaceful coup.

Prime Minister Dragiša Cvetković and his ministers were arrested while Dušan Simović's new government overturned the signing of the Tripartite Pact. A furious Hitler ordered an immediate blitzkrieg attack against Yugoslavia, calling on the Italians and Hungarians to assist. Bulgaria was offered territory so German troops could deploy around Sofia ready to attack south-east Yugoslavia. The Croats were also assured that the Nazis would favour them over the Serbs to get their support.

Foreign Minister Momčilo Ninčić suggested that Yugoslavia could stay in the Tripartite Pact. But the change of mind had come too late and the German ambassador, Viktor von Heeren, was ordered back to Germany. In a final flurry of diplomatic activity, Hungary refused Germany's offer of Croatian territories, so Hitler decided to create an independent Croatia instead.

The German press then launched a propaganda campaign to stir up anti-Yugoslav feeling, dividing the Serbs and Croats more than ever. False reporting of atrocities against German nationals sparked an exodus across the border while the final plans for the invasion were drawn up.

Führer Directive 26 was issued on 3 April and the Germans received a bonus when a Croatian Air Force officer, Major Vladimir Kren, flew to Germany the same day. He handed over details of Yugoslavia's air defences, which would allow the Luftwaffe to decimate the nation's air force.

The new Yugoslavian government signed a Treaty of Friendship and Non-Aggression with Moscow because Stalin was all of a sudden interested in the unfolding events across the Balkans. However, no military assistance was promised because Germany was still the Soviet Union's ally.

Hitler promised the Banat region to Budapest to get Hungarian support, causing disputes between Hungary's Prime Minister Pál Teleki and the

Chief of the General Staff Henrik Werth. Yugoslavia's part of Macedonia was offered to Sofia to get Bulgaria's support, while Bucharest was instructed to keep the Romanian army waiting along the Yugoslav border. Yugoslavia's Serbian Prime Minister, Dušan Simović, appointed Vladko Maček as his deputy, to get support from the Croats. It resulted in a split cabinet because the pro-Allied Serbs wanted to stand up to the Germans while the Croat-Slovene faction wanted to be Berlin's ally.

The Axis Order of Battle

Field Marshal Walther von Brauchitsch's plan was to surround Yugoslavia with the armies and air forces of three nations. The Wehrmacht assembled nine infantry, five panzer, two motorised infantry and two mountain divisions: over 337,000 men, 1,500 artillery pieces, 875 tanks and 740 other armoured vehicles. General Maximilian von Weichs' Second Army assembled across south-east Austria and south-west Hungary, ready to advance into northern Yugoslavia. Meanwhile, General Wilhelm List's Twelfth Army assembled along the Bulgarian border, north-west of Sofia, and General Paul von Kleist's First Panzer Group prepared to cross the east border.

The Italians had divided their twenty-two divisions between two armies, ready to invade Yugoslavia from two directions. General Vittorio Ambrosio's Second Army (2° Armata) deployed in north-east Italy in the area called the Julian March, ready to advance across north-west Yugoslavia and down the Dalmatian coast on 11 April. The Royal Italian Navy (*Regia Marina*) would provide support for the ground troops by engaging the Royal Yugoslav Navy. Meanwhile General Alessandro Biroli's Ninth Army (9° Armata) would wait in northern Albania ready to take advantage of developments.

The chief of the Hungarian General Staff, General Henrik Werth, had promised General Friedrich Paulus that the Royal Hungarian Army (*Magyar Honvédség*) would support the invasion. However, the Supreme Defence Council stated that Hungarian troops had to remain under their own commanders and that they could only be used to occupy territory abandoned by the Yugoslav Army.

Germany said the original agreement was final, while Britain warned Hungary not to allow Wehrmacht troops to cross its territory. As a result, Prince Regent Miklós Horthy cancelled the mobilisation, General Werth resigned, and Prime Minister Teleki committed suicide. The Germans still moved their troops through Hungary, en route for Romania, so the mobilisation order was re-issued and Werth returned to his post. The Hungarian Third Army was poised to advance between the Danube and the Tisza Rivers into the Bačka and Baranja regions. It brought the total number of ground troops facing Yugoslavia to over 750,000.

General Wolfram von Richthofen had organised successful air support for the Polish and French campaigns in September 1939 and May 1940 respectively, but he had faced defeat during the Battle of Britain. Over 800 aircraft would be assembled to support the invasion of Yugoslavia, most of them flying to their Balkans' airfields just a few days before the attack.

The Luftwaffe's force included 300 dive bombers which would be used to carry out pinpoint bombing attacks on population centres and troops on the move. Both Lieutenant General Alexander Löhr's Fourth Air Fleet (*Luftflotte IV*) and *Oberstleutnant* Karl Christ's *Fliegerführer Graz* were based in Austria. *Oberstleutnant* Clemens von Schönborn-Wiesentheid's *Fliegerführer Arad* was based in Romania, while Richthofen's own VIII Air Corps (*Fliegerkorps VIII*) was based in Bulgaria. VIII Air Corps had 300 planes able to switch their support to the simultaneous invasion of Greece. X Air Corps (*Fliegerkorps X*) also had a large bomber force stationed on Sicily which could switch from attacking the Allied convoys supplying Malta to targets in the Balkans.

The Royal Italian Air Force (*Regia Aeronautica*) had over 650 planes poised to support the attack. The Second Air Force was based on airfields in north-east Italy, while the Fourth Air Force was stationed across southern Italy. Another 220 planes were based in Albania, ready to assist the German invasion of Greece. The Royal Hungarian Air Force (*Magyar Királyi Honvéd Légierő*) also had an air brigade on standby. It brought the total number of aircraft waiting to attack Yugoslavia to over 1,500.

German planes started flying into Yugoslavian airspace to test the Yugoslav Air Force's reaction, while the Luftwaffe moved their planes into the Balkans. The defection of Major Vladimir Kren gave the Germans a list of lucrative targets, including the dispersal airfields the Yugoslav Air Force would use after the main ones came under attack.

The Yugoslavian Order of Battle

The Yugoslav Army was divided into three army groups (although Yugoslav armies were only the size of other armies' corps). It may have numbered 1,200,000, divided into twenty-eight infantry and three cavalry divisions, but it had to protect a lengthy border of over 900 miles. Extra units had to protect the Adriatic coast from amphibious attacks. It was an impossible task.

General Milorad Petrović's First Army Group had to defend Yugoslavia's northern territories. General Dušan Trifunović's Seventh Army faced the Italian and Austrian borders, while General Petar Nedeljković's Fourth Army was deployed along the River Drava, facing Hungary. Second Army Group had to protect the nation's eastern border but General Milutin Nedić had no reserves to tackle any breakthrough. General Dragoslav Miljković's Second Army and General Milan Rađenković's First Arm were deployed north and south of the River Danube. General Milan N. Third Army Group covered the south-east and southern borders and while General Vladimir Čukavac's Fifth Army and General Jovan Naumović's Third Territorial Army covered the Romanian, Bulgarian and part of the Greek border. General Ilija Brašić's Third Army covered the rest of the Greek border and all the Albania border. General Dimitrije Živković's Sixth Army was the only reserve and it was deployed around Belgrade ready to move in any direction.

The Royal Yugoslav Army faced several extra problems as it prepared for the invasion. General Dušan Simović may have decided to delay the mobilisation until 3 April, to avoid aggravating the Germans, but it caused chaos amongst the deploying divisions. The General Headquarters Direct Command's defence plan involved deploying close to the borders and the lack of motorised transport meant it would take too long to deploy. Only seven divisions were ready to face the Axis onslaught on 6 April 1941, while the columns of horse-drawn vehicles found themselves vulnerable to air attack by the Axis dive bombers. The soldiers who made it to their positions had to fight with First World War vintage weapons or imported weapons, resulting in shortages of ammunition and spares. The Yugoslav Army also only had fifty tanks capable of taking on the German panzers.

Yugoslavia's northern defences had been placed along the border to protect the Slovenes, only they refused to fight because of their animosity towards the Serbians. The Croatians also refused to put up any resistance for the same reason and the Ustaše supporters interfered with the Yugoslav Army's deployment, even forcing Fourth Army's headquarters to relocate. Mayor Julije Makanec proclaimed an Independent State of Croatia on 8 April, while Ustaše members took control of Croatian towns. The Germans were then welcomed by the crowds when they reached Zagreb on 10 April. It was left to the Serbian units to stop the onslaught and there were too few to stop the German and Italian armoured columns. The Luftwaffe soon had control of the skies and their dive bombers played havoc with the retreating units as they tried to escape.

The Royal Yugoslav Army Air Force (*Zrakoplovstvo vojske Kraljevine Jugoslavije*) was split into two air groups; they were organised into the First Fighter Brigade, the Second and Third Mixed Air Brigades and the Fourth Bomber Brigade. Brigadier General Borivoje Mirković may have been able to mobilise nearly 425 aircraft but half were outdated while the remainder were a mix of German, Italian and British design. It posed complex maintenance and repair problems, while limited supplies of ammunition would leave many aircraft grounded after only a few sorties.

Coastal batteries watched the Adriatic shore while the Royal Yugoslav Navy had a small fleet to protect its waters. It had a flotilla leader, three destroyers, two divisions of torpedo boats, four obsolescent submarines and a gunboat, supported by three units of hydroplanes. There was also a number of river monitors which sailed along the Danube.

The Air Attacks

The Wehrmacht crossed the border early on 6 April, which was Easter Sunday and an important day in the Orthodox calendar. Many people were heading for church when nearly 235 bombers of *Luftflotte 4* headed for targets across Yugoslavia an hour later. Operation Retribution (also known as Operation Punishment) had begun. The 6th Fighter Brigade attacked the waves of planes but 52nd Fighter Group took off too late to intercept them; only twelve planes were shot down.

The air attacks had been coordinated by General Löhr; he had used the experience gained in the bombing of Warsaw the previous September. German aircraft flew in relays from airfields across Austria and Romania. Fighters protected the Ju 87 Stuka dive-bombers as they targeted the Yugoslav airfields and silenced the nation's anti-aircraft defences. Meanwhile, Dornier Do 17s and Junkers Ju 88 flew over Belgrade in three waves at fifteen-minute intervals.

The Yugoslav Air Force only had a few squadrons to protect Belgrade, so the plan was to declare it an open city in the hope that it would be spared. But the Luftwaffe would have no qualms about bombing what the German press was referring to as Fortress Belgrade. Bombs rained down as King Peter and his government joined the exodus from the city. Incendiaries were used in the initial attacks to light up the city for night attacks and over 200 tons of bombs would eventually be dropped, demolishing and burning many buildings to the ground. Around 4,000 civilians were killed and many thousands more made homeless. The bombing cut communications between the Yugoslav high command and its armies in the field, enabling the Wehrmacht to move swiftly across the country.

The Ground Attacks

Twelfth Army crossed the south-east border with Bulgaria as the Luftwaffe struck targets across Third Army Group's front. XL Panzer Corps was driving south-west towards Skopje when XIV Panzer Corps crossed the same border two days later, heading north-west towards Niš. The Yugoslav Army sent reserves to hold the city but the Luftwaffe would stop them reaching it

Once Niš had fallen, four more corps crossed the Yugoslav border on 10 April. Two advanced from Austria and attacked First Army Group, and the XLIX Mountain Corps headed south-west towards Ljubljana while LI Infantry Corps moved south towards Zagreb. At the same time, XLVI Panzer Corps crossed the Hungarian border and attacked First Army Group, while the XLI Panzer Corps crossed from Romania; they both headed for Belgrade.

The Yugoslav Army was being assailed from all sides and was fighting for its life, but there was more to come. The Italian Second Army had started probing the Yugoslav Army's positions on 6 April. Part of it then advanced rapidly east towards Ljubljana on 11 April, while the rest advanced south-east down the Adriatic coast to Dubrovnik. The Italians would advance over 400 miles in six days.

The Hungarian Third Army crossed the north-east border and occupied the border regions of Baranja and Bačka on 12 April. They had been part of Hungary before the Treaty of Trianon (1920) and the troops were welcomed by the large number of Hungarian living in the area.

The Wehrmacht's armoured columns drove fast across Yugoslavia while the Luftwaffe bombed the retreating Yugoslav units. More troops crossed the Hungarian and Romanian borders turning the retreat into a rout in what was a perfect example of Lightning War or *Blitzkrieg*. A small group of German troops entered Belgrade on 11 April and SS-*Hauptsturmführer* Fritz Klingenberg warned that columns of tanks were close behind them. The mayor believed the rumours and surrendered the city without a fight.

The Yugoslav Army's plan, codenamed R-41, had anticipated a defeat and it included a detailed withdrawal through Albania with a plan to join the Greek and British armies. The Third Yugoslav Army and the Greek Army could then coordinate attacks against the Italian divisions in Albania to keep an escape route open for the rest of the Yugoslav Armies to withdraw through. Third Army may have attacked on 7 April 1941 but the Italians had cracked its codes and they sent out a stream of fake orders which disrupted Plan R-41. Third Army soon called off its offensive because the Germans were advancing through Prizren and Skopje threatening the Yugoslavs' rear.

Yugoslav Air and Naval Operations

The Yugoslav Air Force had dispersed its squadrons to fifty temporary airfields across the country following the military coup on 25 March 1941. Unfortunately they had few facilities, while wet weather would make some of the dispersal airstrips unusable. To make matters worse, the airfield locations had been betrayed and nearly half of the Air Force's sixty modern light bombers (German-designed Dornier Do 17s) would be destroyed on the ground on the first day.

Some Yugoslav fighter pilots attacked the waves of enemy bombers while others gave support to the troops on the ground, but it was a one-sided air battle. There were always too few planes to stop the *Luftwaffe* and *Regia Aeronautica* and only eighteen of the Yugoslav Air Force's planes would escape to an Allied airfield in Egypt. One of the final tasks carried out by the Yugoslav Air Force was to evacuate the young King Peter II, his government and the country's gold reserves to Greece. Meanwhile, the entire Yugoslav Supreme Command had been taken prisoner near Sarajevo.

Two Yugoslav destroyers were captured, the third was scuttled by its crew. Most of the small ships were also captured and only ten seaplanes, two MTBs and one submarine would escape. The four aging armoured monitors were attacked by dive bombers as they patrolled the rivers across northern Yugoslavia. One was sunk by a bomb while the remaining crews scuttled their vessels after their bases fell into enemy hands.

The Armistice and Surrender

Localised ceasefires began on 14 April while the Yugoslav high command sent an envoy to arrange a nationwide surrender. General Paul von Kleist sent General Maximilian von Weichs to Belgrade and an unconditional surrender was signed by General Milojko Janković and Foreign Minister Aleksandar Cincar-Marković on 17 April. The terms divided Yugoslavia into four occupation zones which would be controlled by Germany, Italy, Hungary and Bulgaria. The Wehrmacht established a military administration across the Serbian area while Ante Pavelić declared an Independent State of Croatia. The Italians turned Albania and Montenegro into a protectorate.

The Wehrmacht only suffered around 500 casualties during the invasion of Yugoslavia, the Hungarian Army even fewer. The Italians faced greater resistance and most of its 3,300 casualties were suffered in Albania. Only a small number of soldiers of the Yugoslav Army escaped to fight again, while tens of thousands were taken prisoner by the Germans and Italians. Ethnic Germans and Hungarians were released but the rest would be held as prisoners of war for the next four years.

The *Luftwaffe* lost around sixty planes, many of them during the bombing of Belgrade, while the *Regia Aeronautica* lost only ten. The Yugoslav Air Force suffered catastrophic losses, with around fifty shot down and many more destroyed on their airfields. Only seventy pilots escaped with their planes to Allied territory while over three hundred were captured and handed to a new Air Force organised by the Independent State of Croatia.

The people of Yugoslavia were in shock over the swift collapse of its armed forces but the soldiers who had escaped captivity were determined not to give up. The first battalion of partisans had been formed in Croatia at the end of June while the first partisan action was carried out in Serbia only a few weeks later.

The Impact of the Balkans Campaign on Operation Barbarossa

There have been arguments over the years regarding the impact of the Balkans campaign on Operation Barbarossa. Some say Hitler delayed the attack on the Soviet Union until Yugoslavia and Greece had been occupied. In doing so, the Axis secured their southern flank and put a stop to Allied air attacks on the Romanian oilfields around Ploieşti. Most attribute the delay to 22 June to two problems unfolding in eastern Poland. Firstly, it took longer than expected to prepare what would become the largest military operation in history. Secondly, unseasonably heavy spring rains had flooded the rivers making roads impassable.

Whatever the reason, the rapid conquests of Yugoslavia and Greece were good for German morale. They proved that the Wehrmacht and Luftwaffe could achieve great things with their Blitzkrieg tactics, and it had given many more troops combat experience. The battles in the Balkans would have also drawn Moscow's attention away from the real threat to the Soviet Union: Operation Barbarossa.

Germany, Italy and Bulgaria divided Greece between them and then started asset stripping the country. Many died from starvation or disease, while others such as the Jews and Romani were murdered or deported.

Chapter 7

Occupation of Albania and Greece

April 1939 to October 1944

The Italians had invaded Albania in April 1939 as part of Mussolini's plan to take control of the Balkans. The invasion of Greece in October 1940 had ended in failure, leaving the Italians struggling to hold their own. Hitler wanted to secure Greece and a combined attack by the two countries in April 1941 captured the mainland. An airborne attack secured the island of Crete the following day, giving the Germans an air and sea base in the Eastern Mediterranean.

The Occupation of Albania Timeline

April 1939	The Italians invade Albania and Tirana surrenders after a few days
October 1940	The Italians launch a failed offensive into Greece
April and May 1941	The Axis invade Greece's mainland and islands
September 1942	Communist guerrilla groups form the National Liberation Movement
November 1942	The Nationalist National Front guerrilla group forms
September 1943	Italy surrenders and German troops take over Albania
August 1943	The Mukje Agreement unites all guerrillas but only for a short time
Autumn 1943	The royalist Legality Movement forms
October 1944	Germany withdraws and the National Front seize control
October 1944	Yugoslav Partisans help the National Liberation Movement take over

The Occupation of Albania

Tirana had to follow Rome's lead when it declared war against Britain and France on 10 June 1940, even though the Albanians had no desire for conflict. Mussolini then used Albania as a base to expand his foothold in the Balkans, deploying troops along its southern border ready to attack Greece in October 1940. The Albania Army was supposed to have supported the invasion of Greece but they scattered into the mountains instead. Some, under Colonel Prenk Pervizi, even fought back after the Italian offensive ground to a halt.

The Greeks soon forced the Italians back across the Albanian border and a stalemate ensued over the winter of 1940/1. Hitler wanted more than ever to control all the Balkans because he wanted to secure the Romanian oilfields before the attack on the Soviet Union was launched. So he planned to support a new Italian attack against Greece in the spring.

Yugoslavia was invaded at the same time as Greece, on 6 April 1941, and both countries fell in a short time; it also left Albania once more in Italian hands. Mussolini was well aware of the Albanian desire to control territories beyond its pre-war borders, so he annexed Kosovo, parts of Montenegro and the Vardar *banovina*. The borders of his puppet state were then expanded to cover the claimed areas.

By the summer of 1943 it was clear that the Italians were coming to the end of their resistance and the Germans sent intelligence units to plan the takeover strategic locations across Albania. Operation Konstantin began with troops occupying its ports and airfields, to guard against any surprise Allied attacks.

The Italians surrendered on 8 September 1943 and the Germans moved troops in to occupy key positions and secure the country. Hermann Neubacher, the Nazis' representative for south-east Europe, had sent Major Franz von Scheiger to Albania to work with the politicians. The Albanian National Front were allowed to form a Supreme Council of Regency, headed by Medhi Frashëri, to run the country until a High Regency Council was elected.

The National Front partisans joined a reformed Albanian Army to help the German troops and National Front paramilitaries clear the main road between Tirana and Durrës over the winter. However, they faced strong opposition from the National Liberation Movement and the Yugoslav Partisans. Meanwhile the Albanian police and the gendarmerie worked together to arrest enemies of the state. They targeted the Roma gypsies and

Serbs, putting them in camps, while Montenegrin settlers were moved in to replace them.

The war was turning in the Allies' favour in 1944 and the Yugoslav Partisans had helped drive the Germans out of Albania by October. Tito wanted the Communists to take control of the country but the National Front rose up when their members started being arrested. The National Liberation Movement had soon defeated the rebellion and all the National Front leaders were either exiled or executed, accused of collaborating with the occupying forces. The 70,000 strong National Liberation Army then helped Tito's partisans secure Kosovo, Montenegro and parts of Bosnia and Herzegovina.

Albanian Resistance

There had been little communist support in Albania's pre-war rural society. There was little resistance against the Italian troops during the first eighteen months of occupation, but the Albanian Communist Party was formed in November 1941 with help from two Yugoslav delegates. Small groups formed over the winter and their acts of sabotage and propaganda grew bolder until the Italians gave up trying to control the northern rural areas.

Two leaders organised the communists. Enver Hoxha had risen through the ranks of the underground communist cells to become general secretary of the Albanian Communist Party. Meanwhile, Mehmet Shehu had served as a battalion commander with the international brigades in the Spanish Civil War. He escaped across the border when the war ended, only to be held by the French authorities until 1942. He then returned to Albania to fight with the partisans.

The Pezë Conference on 16 September 1942 brought together all the Albanian guerrillas as the National Liberation Movement (*Lëvizja Antifashiste Nacional Çlirimtare* or *LANÇ*). The General Council was dominated by communists and it instructed the Local Councils to attack the occupying forces until their area was liberated. They could then hand over to a locally recruited territorial unit before moving to a new location.

Ali Këlcyra and Midhat Frashëri formed the National Front (*Balli Kombëtar*) resistance movement in November 1942, to fight the communists and to promote nationalism. They opposed the return of King Zog and demanded economic and social reforms as soon as the country was liberated. Members often restrained their actions against the occupying Italian forces, fearing reprisals against their communities. Its anti-communist stance also brought it into conflict with Tito's Partisans.

The Allies considered invading the Balkans as they advanced up Italy and they wanted the partisans to help with a planned Allied invasion of the Balkans. Representatives of the National Front and the National Liberation Movement met in the village of Mukje in August 1943 and agreed to work together to drive the Italians out. However, the two parties soon fell out over Kosovo's future and the disagreement resulted in the deal being called off.

There was a free-for-all after the Italians surrendered in September 1943 and many soldiers joined the partisans. The National Front seized control of the north while the Communists took over most of the south; they both seized the abandoned arms dumps. The National Front feared the Yugoslav Partisans would support the National Liberation Movement, so it made a deal with the Germans. Its members joined the Wehrmacht in the fight against the Partisans, burning villages and executing anyone suspected of helping them. They also forced the Partisans and Chetniks out of areas which Albania claimed across Yugoslavia and Greece. The National Front scored successes against the Epirus Liberation Front but their days were numbered because the Allies were increasing their support for the communists.

Abaz Kupi formed the royalist Legality Movement (*Legaliteti*) in the autumn of 1943 whose members wanted King Zog to return to Albania. Initially the Allies backed the Legality Movement, but they switched their support to Tito's Partisans during the final stages of the war. Tito had many Albanians arrested after the Germans withdrew from Kosovo in October 1944 but there was soon a revolt in the hilly central region known as Drenica. A two-month battle ended in a Partisan victory but armed struggles would continue until Tito's troops took control in July 1945. Members of the Legality Movement then had to go into exile or face imprisonment and execution.

Bulgaria in World War II

Prime Minister Georgi Kyoseivanov may have declared Bulgaria's neutrality at the start of the war but both the Allies and the Axis tried to get Sofia to join them in a rerun of the First World War situation. Bogdan Filov took his place in February 1940. He accepted Southern Dobruja, the region on Bulgaria's north-east border, when he signed the Treaty of Craiova with the Axis in the autumn. Berlin then offered Sofia Greek territories so that Bulgaria would join the Tripartite Pact at the beginning of March 1941. It allowed the Wehrmacht and Luftwaffe to deploy across the country, ready to attack both Yugoslavia and Greece in April.

Bulgarian troops entered both Yugoslavia and Greece after they had surrendered to the Germans. They took over occupation duties, allowing the Wehrmacht to redeploy to the Eastern Front ready to invade the Soviet Union in June. Sofia chose not declare war on the Soviet Union itself, so Bulgarian troops did not have to be sent to the Eastern Front. The Bulgarian Communist Party went further, by objecting to Operation Barbarossa, and its members formed partisan groups in the mountains to fight the Axis collaborators.

Bulgaria was more focused on ethnically cleansing the territories it had occupied. Tens of thousands of Greeks left to escape persecution, particularly after an uprising around Drama in September 1941. Berlin did, however, force Bulgaria to declare war on Great Britain and the United States in December 1941.

The Communist Party joined forces with the Agrarian National Union, the Social Democrat Workers Party and the military Zveno movement in the summer of 1942. They formed the Fatherland Front, and while they may have had different political views, they all opposed the pro-Axis dictatorship ruling Bulgaria and worked together to fight it.

The Bulgarian Orthodox Church protested against the deportation of Bulgarian Jews in the spring of 1943. Tsar Boris III was invited under duress to visit Germany in August but he refused to deport the Jews, arguing that they were fully employed on essential building work. He died shortly after his return and some accused the Nazis of poisoning him. He was succeeded by his young son, Simeon II; a council of regents represented him while Dobri Bozhilov was appointed prime minister. Despite the opposition to the deportation of Bulgarian Jews, Sofia cooperated with the deportation of the Greek Jews from occupied Macedonia.

The September 1944 Coup d'état in Bulgaria

The Red Army advanced across the Ukraine during the Lvov-Sandomierz Offensive in the summer of 1944. Events moved rapidly across south-east Europe, starting with Bucharest declaring war on Germany on 23 August.

It allowed the Red Army to cross Romania at speed, heading for the Bulgarian border. Three days later, as the Red Army was approaching the Bulgarian border, Sofia announced its neutrality. It also instructed all Wehrmacht units to leave its territory. The Soviet Union declared war on Bulgaria on 5 September and Zveno army officers ousted the puppet government so that the Fatherland Front could take control of the country.

On 9 September, the Fatherland Front staged a coup d'état and the People's Liberation Revolt Army took control of the country. As the new prime minister, General Kimon Georgiev, declared war on Germany, Bulgarian Army units were instructed not to engage the Red Army units advancing across their country. Instead they helped cut off the German troops withdrawing from Greece before engaging those holding on in Serbia and Macedonia.

Georgiev secured control of Bulgaria by declaring all opposition political parties illegal. Some members of the Bulgarian government escaped to Vienna before moving into the Styrian Mountains.

Bulgarian Invasion of Yugoslavia

A coup overthrew the monarchist Bulgarian regime in September 1944 and the communist Fatherland Front declared war on Germany. Three Bulgarian armies joined the Red Army and Partisan units along the Yugoslav border and advanced into Serbia, looking to cut Army Group E's withdrawal from the area.

The First and Fourth Bulgarian Armies launched the first attack on 8 October and they had soon cleared Stratsin and Kumanovo. A simultaneous advance by the Second Bulgarian Army engaged the 7th SS Volunteer Mountain Division *Prinz Eugen* along the River Morava, eventually reaching Niš on 4 October. The second phase started the following day and the Bulgarians and Partisans had soon reached the River Vardar, blocking the main German escape route.

The Bulgarian Second Army and the Partisans captured Skopje on 14 November but it kept driving the Albanian *SS-Skanderbeg* Division and the Albanian National Front back until Kosovo had been freed. Tito then ordered the arrest of important Albanians, resulting in an anti-communist revolt starting in the Drenica region on 2 December 1944. The Partisans would fail to put down the rebellion and the Balli Kombëtar joined the fight to stop Tito taking over Kosovo in the New Year. It would take until July 1945 to suppress the Kosovan uprising.

Operation Spring Awakening

Although Operation Spring Awakening took place in Hungary, Yugoslav Partisans and Bulgarian troops fought alongside the Red Army to capture the oilfield south-west of Lake Balaton which was Nazi Germany's last source of fuel. Hitler was anxious to hold onto the area, so he directed the Sixth SS Panzer Army to move from the Ardennes, where it had recently spearheaded Operation Wacht am Rhein (better known as the Battle of the Bulge) to Hungary to hold them. Soviet intelligence reported the move to the Red Army, and the Third Ukrainian Front prepared defences ready for an anticipated counter-attack.

Operation Spring Awakening began on 6 March, but it had little chance of success because Army Group South was greatly outnumbered. The Sixth Army and the Sixth SS Panzer Army launched a pincer movement through the Transdanubian Hills to break the Red Army's line north of Lake Balaton. However, an early spring thaw slowed the advance and strong resistance stopped them reaching the River Danube. Second Panzer Army, south of the lake, had also failed to make much progress. To the south, Bulgarian troops and Yugoslav Partisans fought side-by-side to halt Operation Drava, Army Group E's attempt to cross the River Drava.

The Red Army retaliated with the Nagykanizsa-Körmend Offensive on 26 March and it brought the Wehrmacht's final attack of the war to an end. The Bulgarian First Army broke through Second Panzer Army's line, seizing the Nagykanizsa oilfield west of Lake Balaton; it then advanced into Austria. The rest of the Third Ukrainian Front drove Army Group South back across the border a few days later.

The Sixth SS Panzer Army had hardly any tanks left by the time it reached Vienna and General Sepp Dietrich joked that it was called the Sixth because it only had six tanks left. The exhausted survivors joined II SS Panzer Corps and were digging in around the city when the Bratislava-Brno Offensive was launched at the end of March.

The Second Ukrainian Front crossed the Hron and Nitra rivers as the Third Ukrainian Front advanced towards Vienna. The Viennese were desperate to save their city from destruction, so Radio Vienna declared it was open on 2 April. Sabotage groups then interfered with the German defences while others gave the advancing Red Army units assistance.

The first attacks hit Vienna's eastern and southern suburbs while other units bypassed the city. The focus then switched to the western suburbs on 7 April to draw attention from the units infiltrating the north and east suburbs. The city was cut off by the time Soviet troops reached the city centre. The final act came on 13 April when a flotilla sailed up the Danube. Soviet troops were landed either side of the river and they captured the Reichsbrücke Bridge before the Germans could blow it up.

Most of the Germans escaped and headed for Linz, with Third Ukrainian Front in pursuit. An enraged Führer wanted the *Leibstandarte-SS* Adolf Hitler to remove their cuff titles for failing to fight to the last man, but Dietrich never passed on the order. Meanwhile the Bulgarians had pushed west, meeting the British Eighth Army in the Austrian Alps.

The Austrians had welcomed the Wehrmacht when its units crossed the border back in March 1938, so they expected no sympathy from the Soviets. However, politician Karl Renner was encouraged to declare that Austria was no longer part of the Third Reich. He was also allowed to establish a Provisional Government to run the war-torn country.

Vienna had been left in ruins, despite the attempts to save it, and many of its people were left homeless and starving. The Red Army units which had captured the city may have behaved but the support troops did not; they robbed, assaulted, raped and murdered the Viennese, without fear of punishment.

The Occupation of Greece Timeline

April 1941	German, Bulgarian and Italian troops seize mainland Greece
May 1941	German airborne troops capture the island of Crete
September 1941	The National Republican League (EDES) guerrilla group is formed
September 1941	The National Liberation Front (EAM) guerrilla group is formed
Winter 1941–2	Tens of thousands of Greeks die in the Great Famine
February 1942	The People's Liberation Army (ELAS) guerrilla group is formed
Autumn 1942	The National and Social Liberation (EKKA) guerrilla group is formed
March 1943	Greece's Jews are transported to Auschwitz-Birkenau and murdered
September 1943	Italy surrenders; German and Bulgarian troops take over its area

October 1944   German troops evacuate Greece
December 1944   Troops deployed to stop demonstrations in Athens
February 1945   The People's Liberation Army disbanded

The Occupation of Greece

Hitler issued orders to take control of Greece on 13 April 1941, calling for it to be divided between the three invading countries. German troops would take control of all the cities, such as Athens and Thessaloniki, as well as the fertile Central Macedonia region; Bulgarian troops would occupy Thrace in north-east Greece; the Italians would occupy the rest of the mainland. German troops would also take control of the Aegean islands and Crete, which controlled the entrance to the Aegean Sea.

King George II and his government flew into exile as the final Allied troops were being evacuated from Greece on 30 April 1941. The Axis took control of the country and General Georgios Tsolakoglou was appointed to run a puppet government, called the Hellenic State, to deal with civil matters on behalf of the occupying forces. The administration's initial difficulties related to problems caused by the destruction inflicted during the invasion. But hardships soon increased because the occupation forces insisted on taking everything of value, particularly food.

Field Marshal List initially dealt with military affairs, while Ambassador Günther Altenburg worked with the puppet government. Instructions were issued by Berlin and Rome to Günther Altenburg and his Italian counterpart, Pellegrino Ghigi. They made sure the Greeks paid for the occupation forces and that food was taken from the people without payment. High taxes and an introduced occupation currency led to spiralling inflation. The occupation authorities also forced Athens to hand over a loan of 476 million Reichsmarks, which would never be repaid.

Desperate times often led to desperate measures but anyone caught hiding or stealing food received harsh treatment. Many were executed while others were deported to work as slave labourers across the Third Reich.

The Great Famine

Greece had relied on wheat imports during peacetime but enforced exports resulted in increased food shortages. The Allied naval blockade restricted deliveries, while movement restrictions across Greece made it difficult to deliver supplies to the cities. It left the Greeks at the mercy of a volatile black market by the autumn of 1941. The occupation authorities were warned that there was danger of a widespread famine across the country but Berlin refused to do anything to stop it.

Greeks living in Great Britain and the United States heard about the distressful conditions from family and friends but it was several months before London ordered the Royal Navy to lift their blockade of the Greek ports in February 1942. The International Red Cross was allowed to start importing wheat, while Turkish ships delivered grain to Greek ports. However, government officials and black-market traders seized most of the supplies and what did get through was distributed in the cities, leaving the farming communities to fend for themselves. There are no accurate records of the famine but it is believed that around 300,000 Greeks died of starvation and malnutrition over the winter of 1941/2.

The food situation eased a little during the summer of 1942 but the Greek economy threatened to collapse under the harsh economic measures. Field Marshal Alexander Löhr and Hermann Neubacher were sent to Athens at the end of 1942 and they organised the economic exploitation of Greece through the German-Greek Commodity Equalization Company (DEGRIGES).

A Joint Relief Commission eventually organised food supplies in the spring of 1943. Price regulations and a relaxation of movement restrictions may have eased the situation but occupying forces kept taking stocks. Partisans sometimes tried to steal supplies and distribute them but their actions often resulted in severe reprisals.

The Italian Occupation

The Italians had taken control of the central and southern part of Greece and the Ionian Islands west of the mainland. They were more lenient to the Greeks but reprisal actions were still taken when there was guerrilla activity. There was also no organised action against the Jewish community, which angered the Germans. The Greek resistance would become better organised as the months passed and they controlled most of the mountain areas by the summer of 1943. The Germans took control of Western Macedonia after the Italians surrendered in September 1943. They then carried out atrocities at Cephallonia and Kosin, executing over 4,500 Italian soldiers.

Advancing across open fields towards an enemy position during the Second Balkans war.

Serbian troops escape through the mountains to the Albanian coast to fight another day.

British troops dig in around Thessalonica during the Great War.

ANZAC and Greek troops fought side-by-side to stem the Axis onslaught through northern Greece.

Sepp Dietrich accepts the surrender of all Allied forces on mainland Greece.

German paratroopers are dropped during the attack on the island of Crete.

Dejected Yugoslav soldiers try to escape the Wehrmacht's advance on Belgrade.

A British SOE agent poses with the Greek partisans he is training.

The Chetniks only fought the Axis for a time, soon turning their attentions to the Partisans.

Men and women served side-by-side in Tito's Partisans.

Partisans and a rescued American airman during Operation Halyard.

Nicolae Ceauşescu of Romania (top left), Josip Tito of Yugoslavia (top right), Todor Zhikov of Bulgaria (bottom left), and Enver Hoxha of Albania (bottom right)

Post-war paranoia led to Albania building thousands of bunkers rather than houses.

Tanks on the streets of Athens as the Colonels' regime seizes power.

A cry for help during the Bosnian War.

Children welcome United Nations peacekeepers to their village.

The Bulgarian Occupation

The Bulgarians had taken control of East Macedonia and Thrace (the areas they lost after the First War), giving them access to the Aegean Sea. They then set about murdering or exiling all the Greeks who had settled in the area with the help of the Macedonian Slavs. An uprising in September 1941 resulted in 3,000 executions in the city of Drama, with another 15,000 being murdered as the Bulgarians stepped up their ethnic cleansing policies. Doxato and Choristi are still remembered as the Martyr Cities. Over 100,000 Greeks had left East Macedonia and Thrace by the end of the 1941 and Bulgarians were bribed to move in to replace them.

The Bulgarians took control of Central Macedonia following Italy's surrender in September 1943 but the partisan groups grew stronger. However, the factions often chose to fight each other as the war turned in the Allies' favour, hoping to take control of East Macedonia and Thrace when the Bulgarians left.

Everything changed for Bulgaria when Romania suddenly switched to the Allied side at the beginning of September 1944. It allowed the Red Army to advance to the Bulgarian border as Moscow declared war on Bulgaria. A communist coup seized control of Sofia on the 9th and the new regime declared war on Nazi Germany. Bulgarian troops were withdrawn from Greek Macedonia, but they remained in Eastern Macedonia and Thrace because Bulgaria wanted to keep its access to the Mediterranean Sea.

A strong British presence in the area and a Bulgarian withdrawal from Eastern Macedonia and Thrace resulted in a ceasefire, but again there were huge upheavals. Around 90,000 Bulgarian immigrants had to return home, where thousands were accused of collaborating; around 2,000 were executed.

The Holocaust in Greece

The Germans had gathered intelligence about the Greek Jewish community before the war, so they knew how to deal with it after the occupation. They arrested community leaders and confiscated items from the synagogues, include community lists, as soon as they had occupied the Thessaloniki area. Jews were forced to leave rural areas and made to live in cramped conditions in the city while their homes were requisitioned and sold on.

Jews were forced to do manual work in the summer of 1942, often humiliating or arduous tasks. Everyone was forced to hand over all their valuables to pay the huge fines imposed on the community in the autumn and then wear the yellow Star of David before they were moved into the Baron Hirsch ghetto. In March 1943 they were then deported by train to Auschwitz extermination camp.

At the same time, over 4,000 Jews from across the Bulgarian occupied zone were transferred to camps in Bulgaria. They were told they were heading for Palestine, to calm them, only the transports took them to Treblinka extermination camp, near Warsaw, where they were gassed.

By the time the Germans left Greece, 65,000 members of the Jewish community were dead, most murdered in Auschwitz or Treblinka. Around 10,000 would survive the war: some fought with the resistance, others spent months in hiding protected by their Greek friends and neighbours.

The Germans also targeted the Greek gypsy communities, including the Romaniote and the Sephardi. They were rounded up, subjected to brutal treatment and then transported to extermination camps. Around 60,000 were murdered.

The Italians did not persecute the Jews in their area as the Germans did, but Italy's surrender resulted in German troops taking over the area. By now the Nazis' anti-Semitic policies were well-known and the Grand Rabbi of Athens, Elias Barzilai, destroyed the list of community members rather than hand it over and warned his people to go into hiding. Archbishop Damaskinos told the priests across Athens to ask their congregations to help and many Jews were hidden by Orthodox Christians until the Germans left a year later. The Greek police also ignored instructions to search for the Jews while members of the EAM and ELAS partisan groups helped hundreds more to escape. Many, including Rabbi Elias Barzilai, would join the resistance and help to drive the Germans out of Greece.

The Greek Resistance

Konstantinos Logothetopoulos took over the puppet government in November 1942. He was supposed to oversee the transportation of 80,000 workers to Germany, but protests and industrial action meant the deportations never took place. Ioannis Rallis replaced Logothetopoulos in April 1943 and decided to organise Security Battalions to counter the Greek resistance, particularly as communist elements were on the rise.

SS-Gruppenführer Jürgen Stroop arrived in Greece in the summer of 1943 to take over as the Higher SS and Police Leader, but the Greek police departments refused to cooperate with him. *SS-Gruppenführer* Walter Schimana took over a few weeks later and he formed Security Battalions, putting them to work, driving the guerrillas from their hideouts. Anti-partisan operations increased and they often resulted in atrocities, because communities were accused of supporting the partisans.

Resistance Abroad

Several thousand Greek soldiers escaped when the Germans and Italians overran their country in the spring of 1941. Some sailed from the mainland to Crete, fighting alongside British and Empire soldiers before joining the evacuation to North Africa. The rest escaped through Thrace and then crossed Turkey to reach safety. The soldiers were joined by men from the Greek communities across the Middle East and were organised into the Royal Hellenic Army in the Middle East and equipped by the British.

The 1 Greek Brigade was organised in Palestine in June 1941 and completed training in Syria. It was deployed to Egypt in August 1942 ready to take part in the Second Battle of El Alamein in October. The 2 Greek Brigade was formed in Egypt in July 1942 but it was never called upon to enter the front line. Instead it was assigned to guard duties behind the lines as the Allies advanced across North Africa and into Italy. It had to be broken up following a communist-inspired mutiny in April 1944.

National Liberation Front (EAM) supporters were confined to camps while the reliable men were reformed as the 3 Greek Mountain Brigade. They were deployed to Italy and took part in Operation Olive in September 1944, helping to capture the port of Rimini. They then transferred to Greece, where they helped the government's fight to control their homeland.

Greek soldiers had volunteered for an elite unit called the Sacred Band in September 1942 which trained for special forces operations. They were attached to the 1st Special Air Service (SAS) Regiment during its long-distance raids behind the German lines in Libya and Tunisia. They then trained for amphibious and airborne operations and spent the final stage of the war securing the Aegean islands.

Most of the Royal Hellenic Navy's ships had been sunk by air attacks during the invasion. However, Vice Admiral Alexandros Sakellariou was able to escape to Alexandria, in Egypt, with a cruiser, six destroyers and a number of submarines and support ships. They were joined by sailors who had escaped Greece via other means and they crewed around forty ships donated by the British Royal Navy over the months that followed. Around 8,500 Greek sailors served around the world, taking part in the invasions of Sicily, Italy and northern France, as well as the attempt to capture the Dodecanese Islands. Around 2,500 lost their lives, many of them sailors of the Greek Merchant Navy.

Many Greek sailors were present when the British Royal Navy took over the *Regia Marina*'s warships after Italy's surrender in September 1943. However, many supported the pro-communist mutiny in April 1944 and they had to be interned. Loyal sailors manned the ships until the navy could reorganise, ready to join the liberation of Greece in October 1944.

Very few Greek Air Force pilots and crew escaped Greece in April 1941, but those that did joined the Desert Air Force. Both 335 and 336 Squadrons flew Hawker Hurricane fighters while 13th Light Bomber Squadron flew Avro Ansons and then Bristol Blenheims over North Africa. Supermarine Spitfire fighters and Martin Baltimore light bombers were deployed for the Italian campaign.

Resistance at Home

Greece had a long tradition of conducting guerrilla warfare, or *Andartiko*, against invaders, particularly across its mountainous areas. Small groups of partisans, or *Andartes*, began attacking the Axis troops almost immediately after the occupation, but their efforts were uncoordinated. Early activity involved attacking small garrisons and the guerrillas controlled many rural areas by the summer of 1942. The Axis retaliated by deporting all the ex-army officers, to stop them recruiting, and the guerrillas withdrew into the mountains. Support remained limited due to brutal reprisals which involved the execution of suspects, the burning of villages and the relocation of entire communities.

The most popular group was the communist-backed National Liberation Front (EAM) under General Stefanos Sarafis, and its military arm, the Greek People's Liberation Army (ELAS), operated in all parts of Greece. The National Republican Greek League (EDES) only operated in Epirus in the north-west part of the country. The British supported the two main groups, helping them to demolish the Gorgopotamos railway bridge in November 1942, but a difference in politics meant they did not work together again.

Guerrilla activity continued to increase, often limiting the Axis troops to urban areas and main roads by the spring of 1943. There were few urban operations due to a lack of arms and a heavy presence by the occupying forces in the cities. The Nationalist Defenders of Northern Greece and the communist People's Struggle Protection Organisation led demonstrations in the cities but they often clashed. German military intelligence (*Abwehr*) and the security police (*Gestapo*) tracked down members of both groups, questioning and torturing prisoners to infiltrate them.

The resistance collected intelligence on the occupying forces, sometimes in cooperation with the British special forces operating across Greece. They also helped British and Empire troops escape, as well as Greek men wanting to join the Hellenic Army in North Africa.

German troops moved into Greece in large numbers in response to an Allied deception plan designed to draw attention away from the invasion of Sicily in July 1943. Operation Barclay created a false Allied army in the Eastern Mediterranean, successfully diverting ten German divisions into Greece while the Italian navy sailed into the Adriatic Sea to counter it. Unfortunately it resulted in a major increase in anti-partisan activities and reprisals, disrupting guerrilla activity for some time.

Around 25,000 guerrillas were still operating by the time Italy surrendered in September 1943. Large numbers of Italian soldiers joined the resistance rather than be arrested by the Germans, while the entire *Acqui* Division fought them on the island of Cephalonia. It was eventually forced to surrender and over 5,000 Italian soldiers were massacred.

The National and Social Liberation (EKKA)

Army officer Colonel Dimitrios Psarros and politician Georgios Kartalis established the National and Social Liberation (EKKA) resistance group around Mount Giona, north-west of Athens, in autumn 1942. The first guerrilla unit was formed a few months later but it was soon scattered by the far larger communist People's Liberation Army. A British military mission encouraged the group to reform in the summer of 1943. It signed the Treaty of Plaka with the other resistance groups in February 1944, only to be overrun by the People's Liberation Army a few weeks later. The political dispute had escalated into a full-blown civil war by March 1946.

The National Republican League (EDES)

Colonel Napoleon Zervas formed the National Republican League (EDES) in September 1941 but Komninos Pyromaglou took over command when he returned from exile in France. The military arm was the National Groups of Greek Guerrillas (EOEA) which started operating in the Epirus area in the summer of 1942. Its first big success was Operation Harling, the blowing up of the huge Gorgopotamos viaduct which linked northern and southern Greece in November 1942.

The viaduct had been demolished with help from ELAS and the British but it was to be the last time the two guerrilla groups worked together. British support for EDES created friction with ELAS and while EDES was accused of working with the occupation forces, ELAS was alleged to have attacked non-communist groups. The rivalry increased and occasionally resulted in violence. ELAS failed to overthrow the government after the liberation and instead it turned on EDES, forcing it to retire into the Epirus Mountains.

The National Liberation Front (EAM and ELAS)

The Metaxas Regime had arrested over 2,000 communists when it banned the party in 1936 but many had escaped when the Germans invaded in April 1941. Left-wing political parties formed the National Liberation Front (EAM) in September 1941 and Georgios Siantos took command. Thanasis Klaras (later known as Aris Velouchiotis) formed its military arm, the People's Liberation Army (ELAS), in February 1942, so the communists could start fighting the occupying forces.

EAM grew from strength to strength and its members organised schools, hospitals and food hand-outs. Meanwhile, ELAS increased its strength to 75,000 fighters and they increased their control over the mountain areas. They also interfered with the deportation of Greeks for forced labour across the Third Reich. Meanwhile, EAM members demonstrated against the government and organised the Political Committee of National Liberation (PEEA) in March 1944. It would get one million votes in a secret election organised by the National Council; it was the first time Greek women had been allowed to vote.

The Liberation of Greece

The German troops evacuated Athens on 12 October 1944, and the British III Corps under General Ronald Scobie entered the city two days later. The Hellenic State ceased to exist and those who had run it were arrested, ready to be put on trial for collaborating with the occupying forces.

The Greek government-in-exile arrived soon afterwards but the Greek monarchists, republicans and communists immediately began fighting and they had to be disarmed. Prime Minister Georgios Papandreou resigned and was replaced by Themistoklis Sofoulis as the situation in Athens turned violent. Six EAM ministers resigned and their supporters began demonstrating, forcing Scobie to impose martial law; ELAS units were also ordered to leave the city so peace could be restored. The Treaty of Varkiza activated a truce between the Greek government and the EAM but the Greek people remained divided by politics.

The Axis occupation had left the country in a terrible state and the Greek people facing a long and difficult road to recovery. Over half a million people were dead (one in ten of the pre-war population) while another 700,000 were refugees because hundreds of settlements had been burnt down or demolished. The economy was in tatters because of the huge reparations, while most of the nation's industry and infrastructure had been removed or destroyed.

There were shortages of everything, particularly food, and the United Nations Relief and Rehabilitation Administration (UNRRA) eventually had to step in to prevent another famine. A roundup of those who had worked with the Germans and Italians resulted in 80,000 being arrested and most were imprisoned because Greece was more forgiving towards collaborators than other European countries.

The Greek Civil War

There were three resistance groups by the summer of 1943. EDES limited its operations to north-west Greece, while EKKA was fighting in the east. The largest group was the communist EAM and its military arm, ELAS, operated across most of the country. The three groups initially agreed to assist each other under the National Bands Agreement, which allowed General Sir Henry Wilson to issue directives on behalf of the Allied Middle East High Command. However, the three groups soon clashed. The British supported a royalist resistance group, called Organization X, to oppose the communists, but it stirred up violence between the guerrilla groups until the Plaka Agreement arranged a ceasefire. The fighting flared up again after ELAS overran and then executed all the members of an EKKA unit in April 1944. It meant there would be no further cooperation.

The Allies supplied all three Greek partisan groups. Most of the support was given to ELAS but the British government was concerned that its political arm, EAM, was hoping to take control of Greece at the end of the war. Rivalry between the royalists and the communists increased as the months passed and the two groups accused each other of collaboration. Concerns increased when ELAS seized weapon caches after the Italians surrendered in September 1943.

The Allies then switched their efforts to supporting EDES and even tried to arrange a ceasefire, called the Plaka Agreement. However, the communists were determined to be in a strong position at the end of the war and ELAS went on the offensive against EKKA and EDES. EAM then set up the Political Committee of National Liberation (known as the Mountain Government) to rival the puppet government operating in Athens and the exiled government in Cairo. News of its formation was welcomed by many soldiers serving with the Armed Forces in the Middle East in Egypt and 5,000 had to be interned to prevent a rebellion.

The Allies arranged for representatives of all the Greek political parties and resistance groups to meet in Lebanon in May 1944. They initially agreed to a National Contract which would have them working together under Papandreou's government, but the EAM members soon left after they argued over Greece's future.

Mainland Greece had been liberated by October 1944. The various resistance groups killed or captured 25,000 Germans as they withdrew from Greece; around 20,000 guerrillas would lose their lives in the final battles. The Caserta Agreement may have placed all the Greek partisans under the command of General Ronald Scobie but Britain's support was directed towards the anti-communist forces.

ELAS units refused to hand over weapons to the British troops, while many civilians were killed or injured during demonstrations across Athens, called the *Dekemvriana*, in December 1944. The pro-royalist group called Organization X then attacked the funeral processions that followed, as political and military unrest spread across Greece. The 4th Indian Infantry Division eventually had to be flown in from Italy to restore the peace. Winston Churchill himself flew to Athens to discuss a settlement, but a terrorist threat resulted in the conference being cancelled.

The unrest was soon quelled and ELAS was eventually disbanded in February 1945. General Nikolaos Plastiras replaced Georgios Papandreou as Prime Minister and his government cracked down on collaborators and communists alike.

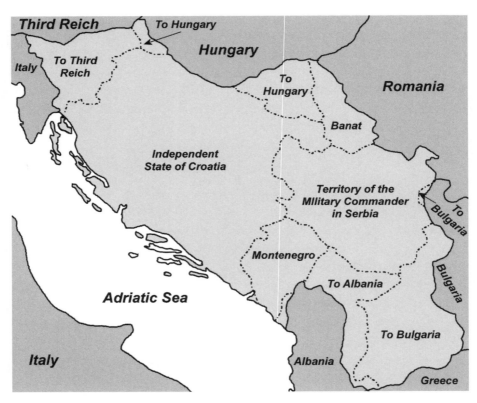

The Axis took parts of Yugoslavia before dividing the rest into the Independent State of Croatia and the Territory of the Military Commander of Serbia.

Chapter 8

Collaboration across the Balkans

May 1941 to May 1945

Timeline

April 1941	Axis forces invade Yugoslavia and it surrenders
January 1942	The Independent State of Croatia's parliament is opened
September 1943	The Italians surrender and the Germans take over Croatian territory
March 1944	Operation Margarethe, the occupation of Hungary
October 1944	The Red Army crosses the Yugoslav border
November 1944	A new government takes control of Yugoslavia
March 1945	The Red Army advances across Croatia

The Division of Yugoslavia

The invasion of Yugoslavia started on 6 April and the country surrendered less than two weeks later. It was immediately divided and the occupying forces used ethnic and religious differences to support their decisions. The border areas were annexed, and while the Third Reich took control of most of Slovenia, Hungary occupied several northern areas. Italy took over Dalmatia, parts of Slovenia, Croatia, Kosovo, Montenegro and Macedonia. Croatia was given territories and it was turned into the Independent State of Croatia (*Nezavisna Država Hrvatska* or NDH).

The northern region of Serbia, called Vojvodina, was again divided into three areas. The western area was added to Croatia, the northern area was attached to Hungary. The rest was called the Territory of the Military Commander in Serbia and was administered by German military governors supported by a puppet Serbian administration.

The Slovene Home Guard

Concerns over the communist domination of the Slovene partisans led to the formation of three groups: the Slovene Legion, the Sokol Legion and the National Legion. Collectively they became known as the White Guards, but they did not attack the occupying forces.

The Italians concentrated their smaller garrisons into larger ones in 1942, enabling the partisans to step up their control of the rural areas. White Guard units countered the threat by collaborating with the Italians, and the Slovene Alliance even recruited an elite group, called the Legion of Death. It relied on Village Guard units to protect settlements on their behalf. The communist Security and Intelligence Service fought back by assassinating several of the White Guard leaders.

In February 1943 the communists agreed to unite their activities against the occupying troops under the Dolomite Declaration. It meant that the Italians would struggle to counter them until their surrender in September 1943. The partisans took advantage of the chaos to seize abandoned arms dumps and used them to kill and imprison the collaborators.

German troops had started moving into Ljubljana Province before the Italians surrendered, under Operation Achse. *SS-Obergruppenführer* Friedrich Rainer was appointed Reich Defence Commissar of the area, while the mayor of Ljubljana, General Leon Rupnik was appointed president of the provincial government. They were supported by SS and Police Leader *SS-Obergruppenführer* Erwin Rösener; he was soon fully occupied tracking down and eliminating the Slovene partisans.

Rupnik suggested recruiting Slovenians into a Slovene Home Guard, or *Slovensko Domobranstvo*, to fight the partisans. The Germans agreed and some were formed into static garrisons, others into mobile battalions and support units. Known as the Domobranci, they initially used Italian equipment but often had to rely on the Germans for ammunition. Many hoped the Allies would land on the Dalmatian Coast so they could switch their allegiance and fight the Germans. The problem was that Roosevelt, Stalin and Churchill had pledged their support to Tito's Partisans at Tehran Conference in November/December 1943.

Conscription at the end of the year increased numbers to over 10,000 and they were soon organised into combat groups. They may have been coerced into swearing an oath in April 1944, but the communists did not forget the oath as they fought each other for control of rural areas. Desertion increased as the war turned in the Allies' favour and SS police units had to reinforce the Slovene Home Guard to maintain their cooperation. Most fled across the Austrian border at the end of the war, only to be sent back by the British. Members of the Yugoslav People's Army separated them from the civilians and took them to secluded locations. Over 10,000 were executed and buried in mass graves.

The Territory of the Military Commander in Serbia

Milan Aćimović was appointed head of the Commissioner Government of Serbia at the end of May 1941. It was only a puppet administration but it was forced to introduce new laws to bring the region into line with the Third Reich. *Obergruppenführer* Franz Neuhausen took control of the area's economy and finances, sending as much money and supplies as possible for the German war effort. He also oversaw the replacement of the National Bank of the Kingdom of Yugoslavia with the Serbian National Bank. Aćimović may have declared that the Serbs offered 'sincere and loyal cooperation with their great neighbour, the German people', however his administration was often at odds with the Germans.

General Ludwig von Schröder took command of the area but he had only been left with a small number of poorly equipped troops. The best units and equipment had been sent to the east, ready to join a new offensive being planned against the Soviet Union. Operation Barbarossa was launched on 22 June 1941 and the partisans started sabotaging military installations on the same day; a few days later they started attacking military units.

Partisan activity escalated over the summer and the Commissioner Government struggled to maintain control of Serbia. General Schröder then died following an aircraft accident at the end July and a plea by his replacement, General Heinrich Danckelmann, fell on deaf ears. It left him no option but to instruct *Einsatzgruppe* Serbia to immediately start reprisal executions. Partisan activity was not the only problem the Commissioner Government faced because tens of thousands of Serb refugees were flooding into the area, from Croatia, Macedonia and other areas.

Danckelmann needed a longer-term solution and he issued instructions to form *Jagdkommandos*, 'hunter teams' composed of soldiers, gendarmerie and members of the Einsatzgruppe. At the same time, over 500 influential Serbs were pressured into signing a public appeal to cooperate with the occupying forces. A plea was also issued for the guerrillas to give up fighting and return home, while a price was put on the heads of those who remained at large. They were also warned that the families of known guerrillas would be arrested and their homes destroyed.

SS-Standartenführer Edmund Veesenmayer forced General Milan Nedić to head a new puppet government, called the Government of National Salvation. He announced that it intended to 'save the core of the Serbian People' by working with the Germans. Saving the people involved sending 300,000 to German labour camps, while another 300,000 were executed in the many reprisals imposed following guerrilla activities. The government also cooperated with Germans when they rounded up the Jews, resulting in most being murdered by August 1942.

The Chetniks may have shut down their operations to avoid the reprisals, but Tito's Partisans fought on. They would eventually force Nedić's administration to close down after they took control of Belgrade in October 1944. Nedić escaped to Austria only for the British to hand him back to the Yugoslavs in January 1946. He was reported to have committed suicide a few weeks later, but it is likely that he was murdered.

The Independent State of Croatia

The Germans appeased the Croatians as soon as Yugoslavia capitulated by granting them their independence. Vladko Maček turned down an offer to form a government to rule with his Peasant Party, so he was ignored. Slavko Kvaternik, the deputy leader of the Ustaše, instead declared an Independent State of Croatia, or *Nezavisna Država Hrvatska* (NDH), which would be ruled by the Ustaše, starting on 10 April 1941. Ante Pavelić soon returned from exile to take control and was accepted as the leader or *Poglavnik*.

Aimone, the Fourth Duke of Aosta, initially refused to be the figurehead of the new state because he opposed the Italian annexation of Dalmatia. King Victor Emmanuel III of Italy persuaded him to be crowned King Tomislav II but he would never visit Croatia and had no influence over the running of the state.

Several German units helped to take control of the north-east part of Croatia, adjacent to Austria and Hungary. However, the majority of Wehrmacht and Luftwaffe units which had invaded Croatia headed east, ready for the invasion of the Soviet Union. Italian troops covered the Adriatic coast but there were soon arguments over their annexing of central Dalmatia. Pavelić defended the move as he had been talking to Rome about it to get Mussolini's support for an independent Croatia.

The Independent State of Croatia formed a 50,000-strong army and the Germans armed it with tanks and artillery so it could help fight Serb Partisans. A Home Guard, or *Domobrani*, was also formed to support military operations across Croatia. Croatia also had a small navy, consisting of coastal craft, to guard the Dalmatian coast and river patrol craft, while its air force took over the planes abandoned by the Yugoslav Air Force. A number of German, Italian and French planes were handed over to boost the Croatian Air Force.

The Independent State of Croatia took control of all the large companies operating in its area, while the trade unions were forced to amalgamate into one syndicate. Berlin dictated how the economy would function and took control of the area's mines, extracting as much as possible for the war effort. A new currency called the Croatian *kuna* was introduced to replace the Yugoslav *dinar*, but money was often printed to finance government projects or lower the pre-war debt owed to Germany. Croatia had to export all its surplus produce to Germany or Italy as well, so Berlin and Rome could control the state's economy.

By September 1941 the Axis wanted Maček to take over from Pavelić. Pavelić retaliated by imprisoning Maček in Jasenovac concentration camp; he was later held under house arrest. Croatia's parliament opened in January 1942 and its first law announced that anyone found guilty of insulting the state of Croatia would be tried for treason and face the death penalty. The minister of education, Mile Budak, summed up the aim of future policies with the following statement: 'We will kill one third of all Serbs. We will deport another third, and the rest will be forced to convert to Catholicism.' The parliament rarely met again, but while the Ustaše had no powers to enact legislation, they did everything in their power to make Budak's promise come true.

The Home Guard continued increasing in size, adding units which specialised in mountain warfare so they could take on the Yugoslav Partisans. Tito retaliated by using informers to spy on the Home Guard units and steal their weapons and supplies. The Home Guard increased to 130,000 men by the time the Italians surrendered in September 1943, but many realised the war was going against them and defected to the partisans. The Croatian Air Force Legion had been fighting on the Eastern Front but it was returned to Croatia in 1943 to engage Tito's partisans.

King Victor Emmanuel instructed Tomislav II to abdicate as king of Croatia when Mussolini was dismissed in July 1943; Italy surrendered just two months later. Nikola Mandić was appointed prime minister but his attempts to include the Peasant's Party in the running of the Independent State of Croatia failed. The following spring Hitler reassured him that Germany was Croatia's ally while he considered Serbia to be a conquered state.

Minister of War Ante Vokić and Foreign Minister Mladen Lorković wanted to switch Croatia's allegiance to the Allies when it was clear that Germany was losing the war. But their plot to oust Ante Pavelić was discovered in August 1944 and the conspirators were arrested and eventually executed.

The Home Guard had to be scaled down to 70,000 to weed out disloyal members, and it would be merged with the Ustaše in November 1944. The new organisation was called the Croatian Armed Forces (*Hrvatske Oružane Snage* or HOS) and its 200,000 men were organised into eighteen divisions. They were given extra training, better weapons and discipline was increased to improve performance.

The Croatians fought alongside the Germans as the Red Army advanced across Croatia in March 1945. Unfortunately the Germans directed all their supplies to the Wehrmacht units, leaving the Croatians short of ammunition, and they were soon falling back towards Austria in a mass exodus to escape the Soviets.

The Allies ignored Mandić's offer to defect and many Croatian units were overrun or forced to surrender to Tito's Partisans or the Soviet soldiers. Pavelić was placed in charge of fleeing soldiers during the final days of the war. Many thought they had reached safety, but they were turned back by British Army units to face the wrath of the Partisan forces. Ante Pavelić may have escaped to safety in Spain, but many of his colleagues were arrested.

Of the Croats turned back by the British, around 130,000 would be executed by the Partisans in what became known as the Bleiburg tragedy. The survivors were held in camps around Zagreb and were treated as second class citizens when they were released. Mandić also reached the British and was handed over to the Partisans; he was one of the many statesmen of the Independent State of Croatia who were executed.

The Chetniks Collaborate

The Germans formed anti-partisan units known as Hunter Groups (*Jagdverbände*). The Ustaše formed their own *Skupine* units. It made life increasingly dangerous for the Chetniks and some units even collaborated with the occupation troops. The British eventually switched their support to the Partisans when they found out. The approach of the Red Army and Tito's offer of an amnesty resulted in many Chetniks switching to the Partisans in August 1944.

The Soviet advance resulted in the Croatian Army withdrawing alongside the Wehrmacht, leaving Tito's Partisans to take control of the defunct Independent State of Croatia. Many former Chetniks went into hiding at the end of the war, hoping to fight back against the Communists, but Tito's security agency, the OZNa, had soon hunted them down. Draža Mihailović was one of the many captured; he would be executed as a war criminal in 1946.

Romania on the Eastern Front, June 1941 to July 1944

Romania shared its border with the Ukrainian Soviet Socialist Republic, an important industrial and farming area. It made an ideal location from which the Wehrmacht could launch its attack. Two Romanian armies (Third and Fourth) joined Army Group South and they took part in Operation Barbarossa, which started on 22 June 1941. Around 675,000 troops would eventually join the advance through Bessarabia, Odessa, and Sevastopol, making it Germany's biggest ally on the Eastern. Romania would receive Bessarabia, northern Bukovina and the region east of the River Dniester as a reward.

Romania continued to conscript troops for the Eastern Front. They ended up fighting around Stalingrad, with Third Army to the north-west of the city and Fourth Army to the south. The Soviet counter-offensive, codenamed Operation Uranus, hit both armies as the Red Army made a pincer movement to secure the city. Over 140,000 Romanians became casualties, and large numbers of their tanks and artillery pieces were destroyed.

Operation Winter Storm failed to rescue the Axis troops trapped around Stalingrad, while Operation Little Saturn tightened the Soviet grip until a general retreat towards Kharkov was ordered. Only a few thousand men had escaped the Stalingrad pocket.

Allied bombers started flying over Romania as soon as the Allies had established themselves on the Italian peninsula. The Ploieşti oil fields became a regular target because they were providing a huge amount of fuel for the Axis armies. Over 175 United States Army Air Force bombers attacked the area on 1 August 1943 in Operation Tidal Wave. However, over fifty planes were shot down in what was the costliest air raid of the Second World War; it also failed to reduce oil production. The Allies would go on to bomb Bucharest's marshalling yards in April 1944 to disrupt the Axis effort in the Ukraine.

The war had ruined the Romanian economy by early 1944, in part because Berlin was forcing Bucharest to send food and supplies without paying for them. It resulted in rampant inflation, food shortages and an unruly population. The unrest increased when the Red Army reached the River Dniester, close to Romania's northern border, in April 1944. Even so, recruitment for the Eastern Front continued until over one million Romanian soldiers were fighting for the Axis cause.

The Holocaust and Ethnic Cleansing across the Balkans

Ethnic Cleansing across Croatia

Hitler saw the creation of an Independent State of Croatia as part of the Nazi plan to ethnically cleanse the Balkans, but *Reichsführer-SS* Heinrich Himmler thought the idea was 'ridiculous'. Pavelić soon agreed to accept 175,000 deported Slovenes into Croatia. Hitler also wanted him to hand over the Croatian Jews. The Croatians offered Aryan status and citizenship to anyone who agreed to fight for the Croatian Armed Forces. The Ustaše were far more enthusiastic about removing Serbs from their territories and would kill or deport tens of thousands of them from their lands by the end of the war.

The Independent State of Croatia issued a 'Decree for the Protection of the Nation and the State' to arrest political opponents to the new regime. General Paul Bader ordered the murder of the Serbs across Croatia, to ethnically cleanse the state, and put Hans Helm in charge. The Germans encouraged the Croatians to arrest and murder Jews and Roma gypsies in line with Third Reich's policies.

Vjekoslav Luburić headed the Ustaše Supervisory Service department which organised the camps and the first one opened at Jadovno in May 1941. Work on a complex of five sub-camps started three months later; they were run by Miroslav Filipović-Majstorović and Dinko Šakić. The special courts arrested so many people that Jasenovac camp had to be established in Slavonia in August 1941. The Ustaše eventually arrested 100,000 people and held them under brutal conditions in the camp system. Prisoners were assessed on arrival and only those able to work were allowed to live. Those chosen to work were categorised according to their 'crime' against the state and identified with coloured badges; for example, communists wore red badges, Serbs wore blue. Work was hard, hours were long, food was poor and living conditions were basic. Men were put to work building the camps under Ustaše supervision and received arbitrary beatings and punishments. Around 13,000 were murdered by various gruesome means, including poisoning, starvation and gas. Women deemed fit to live were deported across Germany, where they were engaged in slave labour. Those too weak or elderly to work were taken to a nearby execution site. Most of the communists and any Serbs who refused to convert to Catholicism were also murdered on arrival. Most were murdered by a just a handful of executioners. The preferred method was a knife strapped onto a glove; the sort farmers used to cut wheat sheaves before threshing.

The Roma and Sinti men were held in the Donja Gradina and Ustice sub-camps. Serbian, Jewish and Romani women and children were held in the Stara Gradiška part of the Jasenovac complex, while woman and children of other ethnicities were held in the Sisak, Mlaka and Jablanac sub-camps. Children were either murdered or sent to Catholic orphanages for re-education and adoption. Roma and Sinti children were usually murdered straightaway; the women were often raped before they were killed.

Initially Croatian Jews were murdered at Jasenovac. But the Nazis soon decided they wanted to deport them to their area of control, and trains were offered after the organisation of the Holocaust was discussed at the Wannsee Conference in January 1942. Starting in the summer, the Jews were gathered at Stara Gradiška sub-camps and then transported to Auschwitz in Poland. It meant the Nazis could rob the Jews of their money before they were murdered. Stara Gradiška camp was evacuated in April 1945. Those who did not die on the journey were murdered at Jasenovac. The prisoners sensed the end of the war was near and turned against their guards on 22 April. Over 500 were killed in the uprising; 84 escaped. The guards then made the remaining inmates demolish the camp before murdering them. It is believed that around 50,000 were murdered in what became known as the 'Auschwitz of the Balkans'.

The Ustaše eventually deported 200,000 Serbs and murdered another 300,000, many of them in Jasenovac concentration camp. There would have been many more victims if the Chetniks had not challenged the massacres and deportations. The Croatians also killed 30,000 Jews and 30,000 Roma, as instructed by the Germans.

Ethnic Cleansing of North East Yugoslavia

Hungarian territories had been given to Yugoslavia back in 1920 as part of the Treaty of Trianon. The German invasion plan for Yugoslavia had the Hungarian armies crossing the border on 11 April 1941, five days after the main attack by the Wehrmacht and Luftwaffe. Ethnic Germans had disarmed the Yugoslav Army by the time they crossed the border. There was only sporadic resistance from the Chetnik partisans, but the Hungarian troops murdered many civilians as they passed through the area.

The Independent State of Croatia handed over the region north-east of Zagreb which had belonged to Hungary before the First World War. The new authorities then set about ethnic cleansing the Bačka, Baranja, Me imurje and Prekmurje regions. Ethnic Hungarian families were allowed to stay but ethnic Serbs who had moved into the area between the wars were held in camps before they were deported to Croatia, Serbia or Montenegro. Hungarians and Székelys (Hungarians living in the Transylvanian area of Romania) were then moved in to replace them.

There was little guerrilla activity across the Hungarian controlled area because there was nowhere to hide in the rolling terrain. Early partisan attempts towards the end of 1941 resulted in many civilians being executed while many more were thrown into concentration camps. Unauthorised sweeps in the New Year led to the deaths of hundreds of Serbs and Jews. Fourteen Hungarian officers were later charged with high treason for carrying them out.

The Hungarians imposed anti-Semitic laws on the 16,500 Jews living across their region. Those fit enough were sent to do forced labour across Hungary while the rest were imprisoned in camps across Croatia or Serbia; many ended up in Banjica concentration camp near Belgrade. That changed when Hungarian Prime Minister Miklós Kállay started negotiating with the Allies early in 1944. Hitler ordered the Wehrmacht to occupy the country in March while he was discussing the situation with the Hungarian regent, Miklós Horthy.

Operation Margarethe may have been a bloodless coup but Adolph Eichmann was then able to arrange the deportation of the Hungarian Jews with the new fascist Government of Unity. They were taken to collection points in Baja and Bácsalmás and then deported to Auschwitz-Birkenau where over 400,000 were murdered in just a few weeks. The Hungarians also deported the Jews from occupied areas of Yugoslavia and they suffered the same fate.

The Red Army crossed the border between Hungary and Yugoslavia on 1 October 1944, driving the Wehrmacht ahead of it. The Germans who had worked for the puppet regime were joined by 65,000 ethnic Germans as they fled the advancing Soviet troops. The Yugoslav communists took control of the occupied area after the Hungarian army withdrew and the Serbs set to work persecuting the Hungarians who had ruled over them. They murdered 17,000 and forced another 40,000 across the Hungarian border in a few weeks. Over 80,000 Serbs and Croats joined the exodus because the communists were arresting and executing anyone they suspected of collaboration.

Tito then turned his attentions to the *Volksdeutsche* (ethnic Germans) who had stayed behind, accusing them of collaboration with the occupying forces. Around 110,000 were held and questioned and over 45,000 were executed or died of disease in custody.

The Holocaust across Serbia

SS-Brigadeführer and State Councillor Harald Turner was responsible for registering the Jews and Romani. They were immediately subjected to rationing, curfews and forced labour, and all adults had to wear the yellow armband. Jewish men were executed as retaliation for partisan activities across Serbia, starting in July 1941; around 30,000 had been murdered in just two months. General Franz Böhme then ordered the execution of 100 civilians for every German soldier killed and 50 for every one wounded in October. The Wehrmacht soldiers refused to execute Jewish women and children so 20,000 were either taken to Semlin concentration camp or a fairground in Belgrade to be murdered over the winter of 1941/2. The commander of Serbia's Security Police and Gestapo *SS-Oberführer* Emanuel Schäfer reported that Serbia was free of Jews in May 1942. It had all happened so fast because the Germans and Serbs had carried out the executions so close to the victims' homes.

The Vojvodina region, at the north end of Serbia, had been divided between the Hungarian and Croatia authorities. There was no extermination policy to begin with, but Hungarian military units executed several hundred Jews when they shot 3,000 civilians following an uprising in January 1942. However, everything changed after the fascist Arrow Cross Party overthrew the Hungarian government in October 1944. Hungarian military units then rounded up 16,000 Jews across Vojvodina. Those who could work were sent to a camp in Austria, the rest were taken to Auschwitz's gas chambers.

The Holocaust across Romania

Romania was complicit in the Holocaust both across its own territories and where its troops operated. Around 375,000 Jews lost their lives, making it the second deadliest participant after Germany. Anti-Semitic pogroms had been policy across the country since May 1937 with the Jews being restricted in where they could work and live. The situation took on a deadly turn when General Antonescu and the Iron Guard established the National Legionary State in September 1940. German troops immediately started crossing the border and Romania joined the Axis soon afterwards. The regime may have only lasted five months but it increased the scale of anti-Semitic actions which the Iron Guard implemented with violence.

Jews near the border were a target following the invasion of the Soviet Union in June 1941 because they were viewed as a security risk. Over 13,000 were murdered, many in brutal ways, while over 5,000 were put on a train and deported. Hundreds died during the prolonged journey while the survivors were imprisoned in Târgu Jiu concentration camp.

Around 300,000 Romani lived across Romania and the Arrow Cross government took steps to remove them. They deported around 30,000 to the Transnistria Governorate, an area of Ukraine east of the River Dniester administered by the Romanians. Nearly half died in squalid camps in what was later referred to as the *Porajmos* – the 'Devouring'.

Romanian troops worked with the German *Einsatzkommandos*, the killing squads which followed the frontline units across Soviet Union, looking for Jews to murder. They helped the Germans round up entire communities so they could be executed or deported, many of them to camps in the Transnistria Governorate. Romanian troops would carry out the Odessa massacre in October 1941 following an attack on their military headquarters. The Jewish community was blamed and 25,000 were murdered in the rampage that followed. Another 35,000 were deported over the next months and many died, either on route or in the camps they were taken to.

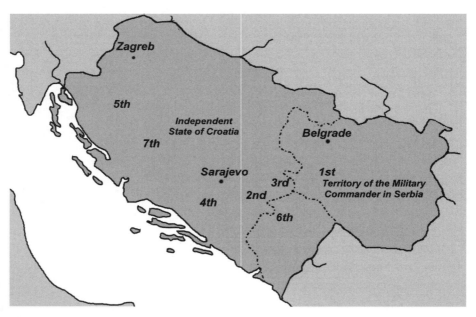

Several resistance groups sprang up across Yugoslavia in the summer of 1941 but the Partisans became the most numerous and most effective. The numbers refer to the seven Axis offensives against Tito's irregular forces.

Chapter 9

Resistance across Yugoslavia

May 1941 to May 1945

Timeline

April 1941	Axis forces invade Yugoslavia and it surrenders
May 1941	Tito calls for volunteers to fight the Axis troops
June 1941	Chetnik and Partisan groups start forming
November 1942	The Anti-Fascist National Liberation Council established
March 1943	The Dolomite Declaration by the Slovene communists
September 1943	The Italians surrender and the Germans take over Croatian territory
November 1943	The Partisans' efforts are recognised at the Tehran Conference
June 1944	The Tito-Šubašić Agreement recognises Democratic Federal Yugoslavia
August 1944	Evacuation of Allied airmen
October 1944	The Red Army crosses the Yugoslav border
November 1944	A new government takes control of Yugoslavia
March 1945	Slovene Partisans join the Yugoslav Army
March 1945	The Red Army advances across Croatia

Three Resistance Groups

Thousands of soldiers scattered into the mountains after Yugoslavia's capitulation and many would form guerrilla units hoping to strike back at the Axis troops. Three main groups would emerge: the Slovene partisans, the Chetniks and the Partisans. They started by increasing their control of rural areas to limit the occupying forces to the roads and towns. They became bolder as the Wehrmacht started transferring units out of the area ready for the launch of Operation Barbarossa, the invasion of the Soviet Union, which was due to start on 22 June 1941.

The Slovene Partisans

Slovenia was divided following the capitulation of Yugoslavia. Germany took control of the north and east, Italy occupied southern Slovenia and Ljubljana, and Hungary received the Prekmurje region. A small area was also added to the Independent State of Croatia. The Germans immediately set about removing the Slovenes. They deported some, imprisoned others and sent those fit enough to work to labour camps. Many of those too ill or frail to work would die in concentration camps. The Italians initially allowed the Slovenes to keep their cultural autonomy but they were soon imposing a similar regime of repression, deportations and executions.

Franc Leskošek (codename Luka) established the Liberation Front and it soon started guerrilla operations across the region. It may have only had a small number of members but they stayed independent of the Partisans, despite Tito's attempt to take them over. The Slovene communists were also anxious to take control of the organisation and they formally announced their intention in the Dolomite Declaration issued in March 1943.

Major William Jones joined the Liberation Front in June 1943 and he arranged the first arms delivery a month later. The number of members increased rapidly to over 20,000 following the Italian surrender in September 1943. German troops moved into southern Slovenia and Ljubljana and immediately implemented severe measures against the Slovenes.

Communist control increased when the Liberation Front committee was elected and even more so after the Slovenian National Liberation Council took over. Further attempts by Tito to take over the Slovene partisans were rejected but the Slovene Partisans eventually merged with the Yugoslav Army in March 1945.

The Chetniks Resist

The Yugoslav Army of the Fatherland (*Jugoslovenska Vojska u Otadžbini*, or JVUO) started recruiting Serb monarchists in June 1941. General Dragoljub Mihailović, nicknamed Draža, formed what became known as the Četniks or Chetniks into guerrilla groups in the Ravna Gora Mountains south of Belgrade. Typically they carried out guerrilla operations in their local area while members of their community supported their activities by moving supplies and providing shelter.

Field Marshal Wilhelm Keitel reacted fiercely to the Chetnik attacks by issuing an order to execute one hundred hostages for each German soldier they killed and another fifty for each man wounded. At the same time, the area commander, General Franz Böhme, declared Serbia a war zone, meaning that civilians could expect the same harsh treatment as enemy soldiers. The Chetniks reacted by scaling back their activities to prevent reprisals against their families and friends. The Partisans kept on moving and fighting, but differences in attitudes increased as the months passed, resulting in the two groups fighting each other over the winter. The Germans were less hostile towards the Chetniks but an attack against their base resulted in Draža Mihailović having to ask for a truce and even offering to fight Tito's groups; the Germans refused. It resulted in the hardcore Chetnik members escaping to eastern Bosnia, while the rest stopped fighting the occupying forces.

The German plan in 1942 was to motivate the Serbs to fight the growing threat from Tito's Partisans, but they were often more interested in killing or exiling Croats and Muslims to create Serb enclaves. They also fought to defend their villages from the Croatian paramilitaries, resulting in the Wehrmacht having to deploy extra troops to maintain the peace. Hitler eventually had to summon the *Ustaše's* leader, Ante Pavelić, in September 1942 and he in turn sacked his Minister of the Armed Forces while giving his replacement instructions to restore order.

Infighting amongst the Partisans increased throughout 1942, as did their tendency to evade the Axis troops, to avoid reprisals against their families. Mihailović's long-term vision had been to build up numbers and supplies ready to attack the Axis when the Allies invaded the Balkans. However, German troops deployed across Croatian territory when the Italians surrendered in September 1943 and set about securing the area. At the same time, Tito's Partisans captured large amounts of military supplies which gave them the upper hand. The Chetniks story of collaboration continues in the next chapter.

The National Liberation Army, or Partisans

King Peter II and some of the government and military leaders escaped the country; many of those who remained behind agreed not to oppose the occupying forces. However, Tito was determined to fight for a communist-ruled Yugoslavia, free from the fascists, and he called for volunteers to fight the Axis troops on 1 May 1941. A Military Committee took command of the thousands of ex-soldiers and communists who wanted to fight and a Central Committee was set up in Belgrade.

The first unit of the National Liberation Partisan Detachments of Yugoslavia was formed in Serbia in June 1941 under Tito. It carried out its first operation in early July and the Central Committee's request for volunteers resulted in thousands of new members joining.

The Communist International, or Comintern, reacted to the Axis attack on Soviet Union by giving Tito instructions to attack the troops occupying Yugoslavia wherever and whenever they could. The Communist Party of Yugoslavia inspired those with republican, left-wing, and socialist views to come together as the National Liberation Army and Partisan Detachments. Tito called for 'brotherhood and unity' and he welcomed volunteers of all ethnic and religious backgrounds. Communists may have dominated the Partisans but they promoted a broad political approach to appeal to everyone.

The First Enemy Offensive, Operation Užice, 27 September to 29 November 1941

The Commissioner Government had been tasked with running Serbia on behalf of the Germans, but a rebellion by the Partisans and Chetniks in August threatened to take over. The Partisans established a republic around Užice, east of Sarajevo, in September, the first liberated area in occupied Europe during the war.

Milan Nedić's replacement Government of National Salvation had to ask the Wehrmacht for help and several divisions were moved in to help restore order. Units of the Serbian Volunteer Corps followed their advance across Serbia, shooting anyone who resisted them. Around 7,000 civilians were shot in just a few days and many villages around Kragujevac were burnt. One of the biggest losses of life occurred at Kraljevo on 20 October 1941 when 1,700 hostages were murdered in retaliation for the killing and wounding of several German soldiers. The following day, German troops and their collaborators selected 2,750 victims after several of their comrades were killed or wounded. They were marched out of the village in groups and shot; the dead included all the boys from the school.

Support for the uprising faltered because Tito wanted to step up action, while the Chetniks chose to stop fighting to protect their families. Instead, Mihailović asked the Germans for extra weapons. His men used them to attack Tito's headquarters on 1 November. As a result, the British officer Captain Duane Hudson advised London to stop sending supplies to the Chetniks before a civil war broke out between the two partisan organisations. Operation Mihailović dealt with the Chetniks but Mihailović refused to surrender his men to the Germans.

The next German push forced the Partisans to abandon the Užice area at the end of November. Only 5,000 would survive the gruelling trek through the mountains to Italian-occupied territory, but they would soon be ready to fight another day. The Chetniks chose to scatter and Mihailović was lucky to escape. They would return home when it was safe and then look to quietly live out the rest of the war to avoid antagonising the occupying forces.

The Second Enemy Offensive, Operation Southeast Croatia, 15–23 January 1942

Tito regrouped his band of survivors in south-east Croatia and renamed them the National Liberation Partisan and Volunteer Army. The First Proletarian Brigade was formed in December 1941 but it had no time to train because Lieutenant General Paul Bader planned to destroy its winter quarters, to stop the Partisans attacking his supply routes across Bosnia. Three German divisions spearheaded the attack while Italian units covered the Vienna Line to the south to stop the Partisans escaping again. The Croatian Home Guard followed behind, securing the cleared areas. The troops questioned everybody, and everyone suspected of being a Partisan, or even helping them, would be shot. Also, anyone who had been away from their village for some time was assumed to have been serving with the Partisans. Any resistance resulted in the entire village being burnt to the ground.

The Germans crossed the River Drina on 15 January 1942 and the Chetniks again chose to avoid engaging them to avoid reprisals. The Partisans took to evacuating villages so the people would not get shot, and burned their houses so the Germans could not use them, before escaping. Rearguards then stopped the Germans following them into the mountains but the Partisans and their followers had to brave extreme winter conditions as they crept through the Italian cordon. Around 1,900 Partisans had been taken prisoner, killed in action or died from the cold.

General Bader soon issued new instructions, declaring that all those who surrendered would be considered prisoners of war. The change in policy may have suited the Chetniks but it ended all collaboration between the Partisans and the Chetniks across Bosnia. The Central Committee of the Communist Party even referred to the Chetnik leaders as traitors on 22 January 1943.

Bader's troops continued to pursue the Partisans between the Bosna and Spreča rivers in what was called Operation Ozren. The Germans again spearheaded the attack, but Tito's men escaped through the Croatian Home Guard cordon a few days later. Operation Prijedor had been started in the Independent State of Croatia at the same time as Operation Ozren. However, the German troops soon found themselves cut off and had to fight their way out.

The Third Offensive, Operation Trio, 20 April to 13 May 1942

The surviving Partisans withdrew south-east of Sarajevo where a Second Proletarian Brigade was formed. Tito welcomed the support of the Spanish Civil War veteran Konstantin Popović as they recruited reinforcements to take control of the Foča area.

Attempts to work with the Chetnik guerrillas failed because they chose a passive approach to resistance to avoid reprisals against their communities. They would eventually collaborate with the Germans and fight the Partisans. Tito's Partisans kept on the move, either looking for new targets or to avoid enemy operations. It meant they did not have ties to the local population, allowing them to be more aggressive, which attracted new recruits. They fought to control mountainous areas, where the Germans and Italians struggled to operate, and then committees were organised to encourage the people to fight or give support in other ways. Tito would welcome support from the Allies once they had seen how determined he and his Partisans were.

An influx of fresh blood may have boosted numbers but a number of Serb Chetniks used the opportunity to infiltrate the Partisans. Bosnian Chetniks proved reliable but they turned out to be poor fighters. Tito soon realised the danger of taking in so many new members, so he organised his best troops into Shock Companies and set them to work sabotaging the railways around Sarajevo.

The Germans and Italians planned to strike back but their counter-offensive was delayed because the Italians were struggling to transport extra troops and supplies across the Adriatic Sea. A premature attack by the Ustaše Black Legion may have scattered the Chetniks but it forced the Germans to advance earlier than planned.

German troops began Operation Trio on 20 April and the Croatian Home Guard again followed up the advance. Rogatica was taken on 27 April and the River Drina was reached three days later. The Chetniks again avoided the Germans, only to be attacked by the Partisans as they withdrew through

Italian-held territory. The second phase of Operation Trio captured Foča on 10 May, but the partisan headquarters had already left.

Operation West-Bosnien then started clearing western and central Bosnia but the Germans struggled in the bad weather and extra troops had to be sent to the area after the Partisans threatened the city of Banja Luka and the Ljubija iron mine. The Italians also launched an offensive through Montenegro and southern Croatia with Chetnik assistance.

The Partisans organised three new Proletarian Brigades after the offensives, while Tito decided to move his headquarters into western Bosnia. They started their 'Long March' at the end of June, abandoning eastern Bosnia to the Chetniks.

German casualties numbered 7,000 during Operation Trio, but 1,700 Partisans had been killed and 500 prisoners wounded. Ustaše paramilitaries helped to arrest thousands of Serb civilians and many were sent to Jasenovac concentration camp; around 25,000 would eventually lose their lives. The Germans withdrew from Bosnia soon afterwards and surviving Partisans soon returned.

The Fourth Offensive, Operation Case White (*Fall Weiss*), 20 January to March 1943

The name National Liberation Army and Partisan Detachments of Yugoslavia was adopted in November 1942, while the new Anti-Fascist National Liberation Council set about discussing the future for post-war Yugoslavia. It was also a significant month because the Allies had landed in Vichy-held North Africa before advancing towards Tunisia. There were worries that the Allies could make a second amphibious landing in the Balkans, so Generals Löhr and Mario Roatta were instructed to secure the area. Many Yugoslavs responded by joining the Partisans, swelling the ranks of the National Liberation Army and Partisan Detachments.

The original plan for Case White was to clear Bosnia, Herzegovina and Montenegro in three stages. However, the operation had be scaled to target Tito's headquarters in the Bihać Republic, in north-west Bosnia. Mobile battle groups from four German divisions spearheaded the advance south through Banija and Bihać en route to the coast. The plan was to cut off the Partisans' escape route into the Grmeč Mountains while three Italian divisions, aided by Chetnik units, prevented them from reaching the coast. The troops again had orders to execute all the Partisans, destroy all the villages and hand over all civilians to the Ustaše so they could be deported.

Tito had planned to relocate his headquarters in the spring of 1943, recruiting reinforcements en route, but Operation Case White forced him to move on 20 January. Rearguards repeatedly delayed the German battle groups and it would take three weeks to link up, rather than the planned two days. It gave the Partisans time to escape but many became trapped in the Grmeč Mountains, so Tito had to send two brigades back to help them escape.

The Germans had again failed to eliminate the Partisans but hundreds of soldiers and civilians had paid with their lives during the escape. The survivors marched through the snowy mountains in three groups. The northern group blocked the Ivan Sedlo pass while the southern group covered the Neretva valley so the main column could reach Prozor. The town was taken on 15 February after Tito issued the memorable order 'Prozor must fall tonight'. A fourth group escorted the medical staff and the wounded to Šćit, knowing that the Germans would execute anyone they left behind.

Civilians followed the Partisans towards Konjic, only to find the Germans waiting for them. It left Tito's men trapped in the narrow Neretva valley around Jablanica. The Germans renewed the attack on 25 February, only to run into strong resistance around Prozor. The civilians were escorted into the Šator Mountains in blizzard conditions and the Partisans followed. As the Germans secured Jablanica and Mostar, the Chetniks closed in on the Partisans' hospital.

The Partisans were surrounded and faced fierce resistance as they tried to break out of the Vrbas valley. Fortunately for Tito, his men had captured Major Arthur Strecker; the offer of a prisoner exchange resulted in a truce. It gave the Partisans time to turn back into the Neretva valley where they recaptured Jablanica. A few men then climbed the ruined bridge and panicked the Chetniks guarding the top of the ravine. They then held on while the engineers built an improvised bridge so that the wounded could be carried across the river.

The Partisans had found an escape route, but they had to abandon their heavy weapons and equipment before heading east across the Prenj Mountains. Rearguards stopped the Germans closing in while the main group recrossed the mountains and the River Neretva. Tito then had all the bridges blown up to make the Germans think he was heading north. But he had his engineers repair one bridge so his infantry could overrun the Chetniks who had followed them. The Partisans carried their wounded across the bridge, under air attack, and then the engineers demolished the temporary crossing. Tito had escaped the Neretva valley but the Battle of the Wounded had cost his Partisans dearly.

Negotiations resulted in a prisoner exchange in March 1943 but the main advantage was a six-week ceasefire which gave Tito time to get his Partisans out of the Neretva valley. Around 20,000 Partisans then marched south-east into Montenegro, taking their wounded and families with them. They sought refuge in the Durmitor Mountains, hoping they could find a refuge where they could regroup, but General Rudolf Lüters was determined to find them now that the campaign in North Africa was at an end.

The Fifth Offensive, Operation Case Black (*Fall Schwarz*), 15 May to 16 June 1943

Hitler instructed the ceasefire to end and General Lüters assembled 125,000 troops, many of them Italian, Croatian and Bulgarian, ready to track down the Partisans. The attacks started again on 15 May 1943, while around 300 warplanes searched for the Partisans' new hideout. One bomb hit their headquarters on 9 June 1943 and while Tito survived, his Special Operations Executive representative, Captain William Stuart, was killed (Tito's dog, Luks, was also killed). Some of the Partisans escaped across the River Sutjeska and headed north-west into Bosnia. However, many were cut off and killed and 2,000 wounded were executed when their hospital was overrun. Hundreds more died from typhoid, but reports of their heroism was spreading, resulting in many new recruits.

The British Special Operations Executive had parachuted Captain William Deakin into Yugoslavia and his reports to London explained how determined Tito was and how brave his Partisans were. What the Partisans needed now was a reliable source of weapons and ammunition.

The surrender of Italy in September 1943 would present many new opportunities for the Partisans. The Anti-Fascist National Liberation Council reacted by forming the Democratic Federative Yugoslavia to rule the six south Slavic republics during its November meeting. It also appointed Tito Prime Minister of the National Liberation Committee and promoted him to the rank of Marshal of Yugoslavia.

The Partisans occupied new areas and welcomed many more volunteers. Deakin also reported the Chetniks' complacent (and sometimes collaborative) stance towards the occupying forces, raising concerns. It confirmed what the British codebreakers were learning about the lack of Chetnik activity from German messages.

The huge contribution Tito's Partisans were making to the war effort was finally recognised by Roosevelt, Stalin and Churchill at the Tehran Conference in November 1943. It was estimated that they were engaging as many German troops in Yugoslavia as the combined American and British Armies were on the Italian peninsula. As a result, the Royal Air Force was instructed to form the Balkan Air Force. It had two primary missions: deliver supplies to the Partisans, and give air support to their ground attacks. Brigadier General Fitzroy Maclean was sent to Tito's headquarters to coordinate the aerial support, under the codename Operation Flotsam.

The Sixth Offensive, Operations Ball Lightning and Snowstorm, end of 1943 and early 1944

The Fifth SS Mountain Corps launched Operation Ball Lightning (*Kugelblitz*) in December 1943, aiming to disrupt the Partisans' winter rest. Search and destroy missions across eastern Bosnia killed around 9,000 but the rest escaped through the thin German cordon. Operation Snowstorm (*Schneesturm*) followed with one group advancing north-west towards the Italian border, the other heading for the west coast. This time British observers accompanied the Partisans, resulting in much publicity for Tito's cause. But again, hundreds had succumbed to the winter weather by the time the operation was closed down.

The Seventh Offensive, Operation Knight's Move (*Rösselsprung*)

Tito established a new headquarters in the caves around Drvar in the Dinaric Mountains and deployed 15,000 of his fighters in the surrounding hills to protect it. He was joined by a British mission headed by Fitzroy Maclean and Lieutenant Colonel Vivian Street. He also appointed himself Prime Minister.

General Maximilian von Weichs, Wehrmacht Commander-in-chief Southeast Europe, wanted to bring a swift end to partisan activity in Yugoslavia. His plan was simple: capture or kill Tito, their 'most dangerous enemy'. Three intelligence sources had searched for Tito's headquarters in the spring of 1944, but they failed to share their information. Front Reconnaissance Troop 216 had found nothing, but the Benesch Special Unit confirmed Tito was in the Drvar area. An SS intelligence unit also located him, with the help of a deserter, but *SS-Sturmbannführer* Otto Skorenzy decided against making an independent assassination attempt after the Partisans recaptured their man.

Tito usually worked in the Drvar cave by day and slept in a second cave near Bastasi by night. He knew the Germans were planning to attack his headquarters and the presence of reconnaissance planes on 23 May made it clear that it was imminent. Even so, Tito spent the following evening at the Drvar cave, celebrating his birthday with his staff.

General Ernst von Leyser was given three days to organise a combined attack on the Partisans' headquarters, codenamed Operation Knight's Move. The plan was for bombers to hit Drvar area, disrupting the Partisan cordon surrounding Tito. At the same time, XV Mountain Corps would advance along the mountain roads to stop any more Partisans reinforcing the headquarters. Transport planes would then drop the 500th SS Parachute Battalion on the target in an operation codenamed Citadel. *Hauptsturmführer* Kurt Rybka's paratroopers would land first with orders to secure the Drvar area. Five glider groups would then land as close to their targets as possible. One would land next to each of the three Allied missions while a fourth would seize the Partisans' communications centre. The fifth would land right next to Tito's headquarters; or at least where the Germans thought it was.

The first wave of paratroopers took the Partisans by surprise and quickly secured Drvar. Civilians confirmed that Tito and his headquarters were to the north, so Rybka ordered his troops towards their objective. The Partisans moved fast to intercept them while a shortage of transport planes delayed the second wave of paratroopers for several hours. Heavy fighting ensued and Tito's guards were able to escape in the direction of Potoci with their leader.

The second wave of paratroopers came under heavy fire from the ground when they eventually jumped over their target and the survivors were unable to break the deadlock on the ground. Milan Šijan's Partisans began infiltrating the German position, forcing Rybka to withdraw his men into a tight perimeter around Drvar's cemetery. Both Rybka and Šijan were wounded during the fierce fighting.

Roadblocks and Allied air attacks had delayed the relief force, leaving the paratroopers to fight alone through the night. Tito ordered his men to withdraw from the headquarters before they arrived and was then escorted away from the danger area. The relief columns eventually reached 500th SS Parachute Battalion on the afternoon of 26 May, having been under constant air attack from the Balkan Air Force. The Germans thought they had secured the Drvar area but the Partisans had escaped along an unguarded road. British commandos then launched Operation Flounced against Brač as a diversion on 1 June. It resulted in 2,000 German troops having to redeploy to secure the Dalmatian island.

Operation Knight's Move had cost 600 German lives. Around 1,000 Partisans had also been killed. But their leader had escaped. Tito's men headed for Kupres and planes then evacuated him and his staff to Bari in Italy. Others evacuated the Allied mission staff and wounded Partisans. The Royal Navy would take Tito and the Allied missions to the island of Vis where they resumed control of the situation.

Tito and his advisors met the prime minister of the government-in-exile, Ivan Šubašić, on the island in June 1944. They signed a treaty to bring their respective governments closer together, by recognising the Democratic Federal Yugoslavia as a provisional government.

The Rescue of Allied Airmen, August and September 1944

Two Croatian pilots defected in May 1942 but they were able to do little against the Luftwaffe. The Germans and the Italians had plenty of planes while the Partisans had to operate without air cover, often forcing them to move only at night. A few more planes were captured but the Partisans had to wait until the Balkan Air Force was formed in June 1944. It would both give air support and air-drop supplies.

Fifteenth US Air Force had conducted hundreds of sorties from Foggia airfield in southern Italy since October 1943, and most had bombed the Ploieşti oilfields in Romania. Many B-17 Flying Fortresses and B-24 Liberators had been shot down over Serbia and some of the crews had survived after bailing out of their aircraft. The Office of Strategic Services (OSS) had been working out how to free the ones rescued by the Partisans since January 1944.

A handful of prisoners of war from Stalag XVIII-D escaped from a railway working party around Ožbalt, Slovenia, in August 1944. They contacted the Partisans, who returned the following day to rescue another 125 men. The prisoners were taken to Semič in White Carniola and then evacuated by Allied planes to Bari airfield in Italy a month later. Around the same time, the US Army Air Force was considering how to airlift airmen from enemy territory.

Dozens of men had been rescued by the Chetniks and they were being looked after in the village of Pranjani, despite German bribes to hand them over. A few of the airmen were guided to the Adriatic Sea but the rest were unable to make the journey, so the Chetniks built an airfield by hand.

The Democratic Yugoslavia news agency in New York City had passed on news of the aircrews to the Yugoslav Embassy in Washington, DC, which in turn had notified the USAAF. Mirjana Vujnovich, an employee at the Yugoslav Embassy, passed on the information to her husband, Lieutenant George Vujnovich, who was working for the OSS in Brindisi in southern Italy. Her message led to the planning for Operation Halyard, or Operation Air Bridge in Serbian.

The British refused to work with Draža Mihailović because he would not fight the occupying forces, but the Americans were anxious to rescue their airmen. The First Air Crew Rescue Unit was organised under Lieutenant George Musulin; he parachuted in to join Mihailović's headquarters on 2 August 1944. Around 3,000 Chetnik soldiers deployed around the airstrip only to be told it was too dangerous to use. So they started work on cutting two more by hand while the airmen were gathered in the surrounding woods.

Transport planes started landing at Pranjani airstrip late on 9 August, while fighters flew overhead; 447 men were evacuated over four nights, ending on the 18th. It was the largest rescue of Allied personnel from enemy occupied territory in the war. Another twenty were rescued from Koceljeva on 17 September and a further thirty-five were evacuated from Boljanić before the end of the year.

The Liberation of Yugoslavia, June 1944 to May 1945

The Allied liberation of France in the West and success of the Red Army's Operation Bagration in the East was encouraging for the Partisans. Tito had declared an amnesty to all the Yugoslav collaborators on 17 August 1944 and many joined his cause. A royalist coup resulted in Romania switching to the Allies in September 1944 and it was followed by a communist coup in Bulgaria. King Peter reacted by calling on everyone across Yugoslavia to support the National Liberation Army, which again boosted Tito's numbers.

The double coup brought the Soviets to the Yugoslav and Greek borders, resulting in General Löhr deciding to withdraw Army Group E from the southern Balkans. However, the Partisans cut the railways in the Vardar and Morava valleys, with the help of Red Army units on the ground and the Allies in the air, stopping the evacuation of 300,000 Germans from Greece.

The Red Army's advance through the north-east areas of Yugoslavia meant Tito could focus on driving the Wehrmacht out of the rest of their country. The Partisans went from strength to strength, clearing all of the Dalmatian coast, allowing the Allies to deliver supplies by sea. The Partisans then liberated Belgrade, with Soviet help, on 20 October 1944, and a new government took control of Yugoslavia on 2 November 1944. Tito then made it clear what sort of future he proposed for the country, stating the communist People's Front would represent everyone.

As winter set in, it was time to tackle the new Axis defensive line across Syrmia. The loss of large parts of Croatia meant that the Ustaše and the Croatian Home Guard were no longer employed in an occupation role, so they were formed into the Army of the Independent State of Croatia.

Tito offered a second amnesty on 21 November 1944, further boosting the National Liberation Army's numbers as the winter weather set in. General Löhr was instructed to complete the evacuation of the Balkans in February 1945, to release troops for Operation Spring Awakening, the securing of the Hungarian oilfield. The reduction in resistance meant Tito sensed the time had come to go on the offensive, so he reorganised his 800,000 fighters into four armies and eight independent corps.

Three regents, a Serb, a Croat and a Slovene, were sworn in at Belgrade in March 1945 while Tito was appointed prime minister and minister of war, with Šubašić as his foreign minister. The National Liberation Army was renamed the Yugoslav Army and the irregular partisan groups were reorganised into regular army units. The Red Army offensive restarted on 20 March and the Germans had soon been pushed beyond Yugoslavia's borders.

Attacks across the Mostar, Višegrad and Drina areas may have linked various groups of Partisans but they struggled to adapt to conventional tactics, after nearly four years of guerrilla warfare. Fortunately, Army Group E favoured its German units when it came to distributing supplies and it left their Croatian allies short of ammunition. By the end of March 1945 many units turned tail and headed for Austria, looking to surrender to British troops rather than the Partisans or the Red Army.

Tito's Second Army reached Sarajevo on 6 April as the Chetniks made a final attempt to establish their status. It ended with their destruction near Banja Luka. A few days later, First Army broke the Syrmian front as Third Army crossed the River Drava and crossed into Austria. Sarajevo fell on 15 April, cutting the Germans' final escape route, while the Fourth Army entered Trieste on 1 May a few hours before the western Allies.

The German surrender came into effect on 8 May and General Löhr signed Army Group E's surrender in Topolšica, Slovenia, the following day. Sporadic fighting followed as tens of thousands of refugees mingled with the German and Croatian soldiers desperate to escape the wrath of the Soviet troops and the Partisans. Over 400,000 refugees gathered in Zagreb alone. The Partisans fought the last Croatian units around Poljana on 15 May, but the last battle of the war in Europe came to an end around Odžak on 25 May 1945.

The end of the war did not signify a return to peace for the Yugoslav people; it marked the start of reprisals. The Partisans singled out anyone who had fought for, or who had collaborated with, the occupying forces and executed them. Huge columns of soldiers and civilians were soon heading towards the border, fearing for their lives, despite Tito's offers of an amnesty if they surrendered. Those who did reach the British troops along the Italian border were turned back and many were executed while the rest were imprisoned. The situation became so volatile that Tito had to issue orders to stop the mass murders on 14 May. Instead, all the prisoners would be held until they could be brought before a military court. It was the start of a thirty-five year period of oppressive communism rule.

Naval Campaigns off the Balkan Coast

The Italians had controlled the Balkan coast since April 1941, driving the Royal Navy out of the Adriatic. Yugoslav Partisans started assembling a small flotilla of fishing boats in September 1942; they would add nearly 250 warships, patrol boats and support ships over the next twelve months. They also seized a number of coastal batteries and islands from the occupying forces. The British wanted to take advantage of the Italian surrender in September 1943, with a view to establishing a base in the Adriatic. They Royal Navy looked to the Partisans for help as they gained control of the sea and attacked German shipping.

General Rommel launched Operation Downpour (*Wolkenbruch*), which drove the Partisans from the northern Adriatic coast. Then came Operation Autumn Storm (*Herbstgewitter*), which took control of all the islands. Only Vis, near Split, remained out of their grasp, and the Royal Navy took Tito to it following the German attempt to capture his headquarters (Operation Knight's Move). He would stay there until Belgrade was liberated at the end of 1944.

The British considered making an amphibious landing on the mainland to support the Partisans by launching Operation Gelignite against Istria and Operation Armpit against Dalmatia. However, both the Americans and Tito opposed landing troops, so the Balkan Air Force was organised to support guerrilla operations instead. The only amphibious operation carried out in the area was Operation Antagonise, an attack against the naval base on Lošinj island, south-east of the Istrian peninsula, in December 1944.

The Germans had lost most of their warships by the end of October 1944. It was left to a flotilla of merchant ships to evacuate several thousand Germans from Trieste and the Istrian peninsula at the end of the war. They were taken to a harbour east of Venice and into British hands.

The Partisans' equipment and civilian support

The Partisans used arms caches abandoned by the Yugoslav Army to begin with. Later they became skilled at stealing weapons and ammunition from Axis arms depots and supply columns. Workshops were set up to copy all kinds of weapons, while Great Britain and the Soviet Union delivered supplies to the Partisans at various stages in the war. The largest boost to their munitions dumps occurred when the Italians surrendered in September 1943.

The National Liberation Movement became popular with the people of Yugoslavia and six million civilians would eventually support its cause. They became involved in a wide variety of support roles, even though they risked being arrested and shot. Some provided shelter and food, sometimes looking after wounded Partisans, while others moved arms and ammunition to where it was needed most. Even more provided intelligence information, helping the Partisans to both avoid and attack the occupying forces.

The communists supported women's rights and encouraged them to support the cause any way they could to help drive out the occupying forces. Two million women would eventually join the Anti-Fascist Women's Front. They tended the wounded in makeshift hospitals, taught children in underground schools and worked for the local communist committees. Many military units accepted women members and they often served alongside men in combat. Eventually around 100,000 women would serve in the National Liberation Army. However, gender equality disappeared when the fighting ended and women were expected to return to their traditional role of taking care of the family and home in the post-war era.

A Summary of the Partisans

Tito's Partisans were one of the most (if not the most) effective resistance groups across Axis-occupied Europe in the war. Over four years they had grown from a few isolated bands of guerrillas into a huge army which drove the invaders from their country. Time and again they had raided enemy installations and sabotaged supply routes before slipping away to their mountain hideaways. They had fought off troops backed up by tanks, artillery and planes with their limited supplies of arms and ammunition. They had endured arduous marches across mountains in atrocious weather, knowing they faced torture and execution if they were captured, even if they had been wounded.

The number of casualties increased as the National Liberation Army grew in size. Around 5,000 Partisans lost their lives every month throughout 1941 and 1942 and that number had doubled by 1943. The huge expansion in the number of Partisan groups following Italy's surrender and Tito's amnesty resulted in the number of casualties increasing further. Over 240,000 lost their lives in 1944, and nearly 220,000 died driving the occupying forces out in the final months of the war. Altogether, over 700,000 men and women died fighting for the Partisans, but the dying did not end with the liberation of Yugoslavia.

Romania joins the Allies, August 1944 to May 1945

The Red Army had reached Romania's northern border by April 1944 but Moscow then switched its attentions to Army Group Centre. Operation Bagration was launched in July 1944 and once it had broken the German line the Soviets turned their attentions back to Romania. German intelligence foolishly dismissed Romanian suggestions of an imminent attack against Moldavia on its north-east border. Army Group South Ukraine was taken by surprise when the Second and Third Ukrainian Fronts launched the Jassy-Kishinev Offensive on 20 August 1944. The collapse of the Romanian Third Army would allow the Red Army to destroy the Sixth German Army in just three days.

The disaster inspired King Michael I to stage a coup and it removed the dictator Ion Antonescu. The German ambassador Manfred von Killinger refused an offer to let the Wehrmacht leave the country unmolested, so Michael issued a ceasefire. He then offered Romanian's services to the Allies and declared war on Nazi Germany on 23 August.

The Romanians stopped the Germans from seizing Bucharest and there was fierce fighting as they were driven out of their country. Red Army units joined the fight for Transylvania, helping to capture over 50,000 German prisoners, and an armistice was eventually signed on 12 September 1944. Romanian units then drove the German garrisons from the Ploieşti oilfields before joining the Red Army in the advance through Hungary and Yugoslavia. Over 500,000 Romanian soldiers would end up fighting Austria and Czechoslovakia by the end of the war in Europe; around 167,000 were killed or wounded.

Stalin had been happy to accept Romania's help during the final months of the war but the Romanian people were going to suffer for fighting alongside the Germans for three years. The country's future had been decided when Prime Minister Winston Churchill agreed to Stalin's request for control of the nation, at a conference in Moscow in October 1944. Over 130,000 soldiers would be deported to the Soviet Union to work as a punishment, while their families and friends faced twelve years of Red Army occupation.

The Allies acknowledged that Romania had been an ally of Germany when it considered its role in the war at the Treaty of Paris in 1947. It was forced to pay reparations to the Soviet Union as a penalty for its actions. But the Allies also recognised that Romania had spent the last nine months fighting the Axis. So Bucharest was given control of Northern Transylvania, the area it had lost to Hungary under the 1940 Second Vienna Award.

The spread of communism across the Balkan states in the post-war years was rapid. Meanwhile, Greece was engulfed in a civil war between the nationalists and the communists.

Chapter 10

Post-war Extremism

April 1945 to March 1953

The Post-occupation Timeline

April 1945	German troops fall back into Austria
8 May 1945	The Second World War ends
15 May	The march back into Yugoslavia starts, followed by mass executions
November 1945	The Communist Party win a rigged election in Yugoslavia
November 1945	Georgi Dimitrov becomes head of the Bulgarian Fatherland Front
November 1946	The Communists win a rigged election in Romania
January 1946	The People's Assembly takes control of Albania and abolishes the monarchy
September 1946	Bulgaria's monarchy is abolished and a People's Republic is declared
March 1947	The Greek Civil War restarts
June 1948	Yugoslavia is expelled from the Communist Information Bureau
October 1949	The Greek Civil War ends
March 1953	Stalin dies and Georgy Malenkov takes over the Soviet Union

Repatriations and Reprisals across Yugoslavia

Since May 1944 the People's Protection Department (OZNa) and the People's Defence Force had been working together across Yugoslavia to arrest those who had collaborated with the Nazis. Their main targets were the Serbs who had fought with the Chetniks and the Croatians who had served in the Ustaše. Mladen Lorković and Ante Vokić had plotted to assassinate the head of the Ustaše, Ante Pavelić, in August 1944, with a view to opening negotiations with the Allies. However, their attempt failed and the plotters were arrested and executed at the end of the war.

The Red Army had advanced quickly across Romania and Hungary to the border of Yugoslavia in August and September 1944. It then helped the Partisans drive the Germans and Milan Nedić's supporters out of Serbia. Tito had offered amnesties to the Chetniks, boosting the Partisans' numbers, while members of the Croatian and Slovene Home Guards helped his men drive out the Germans and their collaborators.

The Yugoslav People's Army had expanded to around 800,000 members by early 1945 and it had massive support from the population. The whole of Bosnia and Herzegovina and Slavonia was cleared in April, leaving only the Zagreb area under the control of the Wehrmacht and the Croatian Armed Forces; they were also supported by the 40,000 Russians of the XV SS Cossack Cavalry Corps.

The German front between the Danube and Sava rivers collapsed in April 1945. They headed for the Austrian border hoping to surrender to the British rather than face the Red Army or the Partisans. Members of the recently formed Montenegrin National Army were heading in the same direction. Tens of thousands of civilians joined the exodus; the Allies wondered if the Ustaše were using them as human shields, but they too were fleeing the wrath of the Partisans.

Nazi Germany surrendered unconditionally on 7 May 1945 and all military activity ceased the following day. General Löhr handed control of the Ustaše over to Pavelić and then surrendered the Wehrmacht's Army Group E to the Allies. Meanwhile the Partisans were busy liberating Zagreb, executing anyone who chose to oppose them, as Tito called for all armed collaborators to stop fighting and surrender.

Partisan units had blocked the escape route at Maribor and Celje, but tens of thousands of soldiers and civilians had still reached Dravograd. Bulgarian troops stopped them crossing the River Drava while those who headed for Prevalje and Bleiburg were attacked by the Partisans. Some managed to break through the cordon and they were relieved to reach the British troops stationed around Bleiburg.

The chaotic retreat had left around 200,000 troops and civilians stretched out on the roads of north-west Yugoslavia. Representatives from the British Army, the Yugoslav Army and the Croatian Defence Forces met in Bleiburg Castle to decide what to do with them. The Croatians wanted to surrender to the British but they were told they would have to cooperate with the Yugoslav military. Unfortunately some of the Partisans fired into the crowds causing mass panic before the surrender could be arranged. The volatile situation eventually eased when Tito ordered the Partisans to withdraw from the border area on 21 May.

Some soldiers and civilians had escaped across the Loibl Pass but the Partisans blocked their escape route across the Drava at Hollenburg. The British rounded up the few who crossed the river and they were escorted to Viktring camp near Klagenfurt. They were told they were going to be moved to camps in Italy when in actual fact they were directed to Bleiburg.

The 40,000 Russian Cossacks were the only organised body of troops who managed to cross the border into Austria, where they surrendered to British forces. They were promised safe custody, unaware that Churchill and Roosevelt had agreed to Stalin's request to repatriate them to the Soviet Union at the recent Yalta Conference. A few escaped but the rest were handed over to members of the Soviet counter-intelligence organisation, SMERSH. They would spend several years in the Soviet prison system, the dreaded Gulag, and many would perish.

The March back into Yugoslavia

The Croatian Defence Forces agreed to surrender on 15 May and their members gathered at Bleiburg, where they were disarmed. A forced march across Slovenia followed and those too weak to keep up with the crowds were shot. The survivors were taken to camps along the Drava River where soldiers were identified so they could be taken to one of the killing sites around Maribor and Celje; over 130,000 would be executed in just a few days. The rest were marched to Samobor on the Croatian border before they were held in temporary camps around Zagreb prior to release.

Intelligence chief Aleksandar Ranković instructed the People's Defence Corps and the People's Protection Department to complete the murder operation as soon as possible. So thousands of prisoners were marched to Jesenice, Celje, Kočevski Rog and Barbara coal mine. There they were executed and their bodies dumped in abandoned mine shafts, quarry pits and caves rather than burying them.

The rest of the prisoners (around 175,000) had been relocated to camps across Croatia and Vojvodina by 12 June. Deputy Prime Minister of Yugoslavia, Edvard Kardelj, wanted them all dead and gave instructions to kill as many as possible before an amnesty was introduced on 3 August.

His execution teams were nearly successful: only 40,000 survived. Although they were released, many were rearrested and forced to do manual labour. They were finally released in the spring of 1946, but they were still kept under observation by the People's Protection Department.

Transports of Serbs and Montenegrins had followed the Croatians, but the movement of Slovenes across the border was stopped when news of the massacres had leaked out. It brought an end to the repatriations from Allied-held territory.

The massacres were kept secret after the war. Documents were classified, execution locations and burial sites were hidden and memorial ceremonies were banned. Relatives of the victims continued to be victimised by the regime for many years after the war, while tens of thousands more had to escape Yugoslavia to avoid persecution.

The Post-war Purges

Yugoslavia may have been liberated but Tito and his communist comrades wanted to purge the nation of real and suspected enemies. That involved murdering or deporting Germans and Hungarians, as well as collaborators of the old regime and opponents of the new one.

Around half a million ethnic Germans, or *Volksdeutsche*, had been living in Yugoslavia but tens of thousands had fled as the Red Army and the Partisans advanced across the country in the autumn of 1944. Tito placed Brigadier General Ivan Rukavina in control of the liberated areas and he initially set about rounding up all the Serbs who had collaborated with the Germans and the Chetniks. He also targeted members of the Serbian intelligentsia and around 24,000 people would be executed in a few weeks. Tito included members of Serbia's Government of National Salvation in the round-up and only one member of General Nedić's regime would survive.

Rukavina's next target was the 200,000 ethnic Germans who had not fled and hundreds were executed. The survivors had their citizenship cancelled and while rich families were offered the chance to buy theirs back, the rest became subjects of the state who faced having their properties and possessions confiscated. The authorities also persecuted the ethnic Hungarians who had settled in north-east Serbia between the wars because they were suspected of collaborating with the Nazis; around 25,000 were executed.

Most surviving German and Hungarian adults were held in camps and made to do forced labour; nearly 50,000 would die from overwork, malnutrition and disease. The youngest children were taken from their parents and handed to Slavs to raise; many would never see their families again. The Soviets also deported thousands, many of them women, to work in Siberia or the Ukraine; most would never return. The bloodshed continued for months after the war and thousands more had been murdered by the time the camps closed in March 1948. The few ethnic Germans still left alive in Yugoslavia continued to be persecuted and most had left for Germany by 1950.

The Department for People's Protection or OZNa

Aleksandar Ranković (codename Marko) had organised the Department for People's Protection in May 1944 to coordinate intelligence and security functions across occupied Yugoslavia. OZNa (the acronym of *Odjeljenje za Zaštitu Naroda*) observed those who collaborated with the occupying forces and noted anyone who spoke out against communist ideals, ready to take action when the Germans had been driven out.

The National Liberation Army's role changed to securing areas liberated by the Red Army and the Partisans during the final weeks of the war. It also changed its name to the Yugoslav People's Army and formed its intelligence branch which worked to prevent the sabotage of military installations. OZNa continued tracking down enemies of the state and infiltrating opposition political groups both at home and abroad.

Around 1.7 million Yugoslavians had died in the war and many more were refugees who had lost their homes. Much of the violence had been caused by ethnic rivalries, such as the Serbs and Croats who murdered rivals or forced them to leave their respective territories. Altogether one million Yugoslav casualties had resulted from ethnic cleansing and partisan rivalries and it would take a strong leader to unite the nation again.

Tito was hesitant to include the exiled King Peter II in the running of a post-war Yugoslavia but he eventually accepted that a Regency Council could represent the King in February 1945. In return, Peter gave the Council powers to establish an interim government, with Tito at its head. An election was set for 11 November 1945, and while the pre-war parties reformed, the majority supported Tito. Despite the healthy support, the Communists felt the need to ban newspapers and threaten party leaders, to make them withdraw from campaigning. A secret ballot had been promised, but voters had to place slips in boxes allocated to each party while OZNa agents looked on. Dissenters would later be arrested.

The monarchists boycotted the rigged election, which only increased the Communist Party victory. Tito was appointed Prime Minister and Minister of Foreign Affairs on 29 November 1945, while the exiled King Peter II was deposed. The new Federal People's Republic of Yugoslavia was divided into six People's Republics: Slovenia, Serbia, Croatia, Bosnia and Herzegovina, Montenegro and Macedonia. Regional governments may have administered each republic but all received their instructions from the central government based in Belgrade.

Opposition parties, such as the Croatian Peasant's Party, were banned and their members were arrested. The civilian and military parts of OZNa separated in March 1946 as the country looked forward to peacetime, albeit it one under surveillance. The civilian section was renamed the State Security Administration or UDBA (the acronym for *Uprava Državne Bezbednosti*), while the army's section was called the Army Security Administrative or KOS (the acronym for *Kontra Obavještanja Služba*).

UDBA was organised into districts and initially focused on arresting political opponents to Yugoslavia's new regime. It then became involved in the kidnapping or assassination of those who continued to oppose Tito's government from abroad. At the same time, KOS was collecting information on behalf of the armed forces.

The UDBA had central units based in the six republic capitals, while mobile groups moved between towns and rural areas to maintain state security. They used agents to monitor the press, they checked all forms of communication, everyone and everything crossing the border, and they spied on citizens and foreign visitors alike. Individuals were often arrested without reason, their houses searched, their mail read and their telephones tapped.

The Crusaders and Operation Guardian

Some of the members of the Ustaše, the Croatian Home Guard and the Croatian legionnaires who returned home after the war, decided to resist the communist regime. They formed guerrilla groups and called themselves the *Križari* – Crusaders. Some sabotaged government buildings or railways, others tried to assassinate state officials or party members.

Major Ante Vrban visited the Crusaders in 1946 and Lovro Sučić and Božidar Kavran used his report to plan an uprising, codenamed Operation 10 April (the anniversary of the proclamation of the Independent State of Croatia) with American and British help. The first group returned home after failing to locate any of the Crusaders in June, but the UDBA had learnt of the mission. It planned to stop future attempts with Operation Guardian (*Gvardijan*), Kavran's codename. A UDBA agent contacted Ante Vrban and Ljubo Miloš in Austria about a fake Crusader group; the group which went in search of it was arrested. Miloš and Vrban confessed to being the commanders of the Jasenovac and Stara Gradiška concentration camps under interrogation and agreed to cooperate with the UDBA.

With the help of codes and Miloš's signature, false messages reported the mission's success. Kavran sent more groups into Yugoslavia and he went with the last group. They were all taken prisoner; all ninety-six men would be tried and executed in August 1948.

The authorities were always concerned that many more members of the exiled Ustaše would return, so the OZNa made great efforts to track the Crusader groups down so that the People's Defence Force could eliminate them. Eventually the government used an amnesty to trick many into surrendering. They were executed or imprisoned and their families and supporters were exiled to the Adriatic islands. The People's Army and OZNa had eliminated most of the Crusader groups by 1947 and the organisation was disbanded.

Consolidating Control

Tito wanted Yugoslavia to expand its control over the Balkans and it coordinated its economic plans, industrial output and trade deals with Bulgaria and Albania. He also wanted to turn Bulgaria into another federal republic, so Yugoslav and Bulgarian delegations went to Moscow to discuss terms. Stalin and his Minister of Foreign Affairs, Vyacheslav Molotov, wanted to direct the merger, and the Yugoslav delegates headed home after seeing how much control Moscow had over Sofia. Yugoslavia also wanted to turn the People's Republic of Albania from a satellite into a federal republic. However, Tito distrusted the Albanian leader, Enver Hoxha, and even tried to remove him from power.

Tito allied with the Soviet Union and the nation demonstrated its anti-Western stance when two American aeroplanes were shot down while flying through Yugoslav airspace in August 1946. Yugoslavia may have joined the Soviet Union in supporting the communists in the Greek civil war, but Tito refused to let it become a satellite state. Moscow sent a letter to Belgrade in March 1948 which said the Yugoslavs were being disrespectful and that they had to remove 'dubious Marxists' from the government. Tito refused.

A second letter from Moscow pointed out Yugoslavia's differences from the Soviet social and economic systems. It also claimed that the Red Army had single-handedly saved the country from the Germans. This may have been the case for other Eastern Bloc countries, but Tito's reply correctly pointed out that the Partisans had played an important part in driving the Germans and Italians out of Yugoslavia.

Moscow blamed Tito and his deputy Edvard Kardelj for the animosity between the two countries. It supported Andrija Hebrang and Sreten Žujović, so they were expelled from the Communist Party. Tito was told to attend a meeting of the Communist Information Bureau, or Cominform, (*Informbiroin* in Serbo-Croatian) on 28 June to discuss the matter. The date had been chosen because it was an important anniversary of three events in the Yugoslav calendar:

The success over the Ottomans at the Battle of Kosovo Field in 1389.

The assassination of Archduke Franz Ferdinand in Sarajevo in 1914.

The adoption of the Vidovdan Constitution in 1921.

Tito wisely said he was too ill to attend, knowing that he could be arrested, tried and executed for defying Moscow. So Yugoslavia was expelled from the Cominform and accused of embracing capitalism. It marked the start of a seven-year silence between Moscow and Belgrade, known as the Informbiro Period, which left Yugoslavia isolated. A side-effect of the split was that the Greek communists refused to accept Yugoslavian aid; it would disrupt their cause and they had been defeated by 1949.

The State Security Administration (UDBA) arrested anyone who rebelled against the anti-Soviet stance, while Moscow ramped up the pressure against Belgrade. Red Army troops deployed close to Yugoslavia's northern border alongside the recently mobilised Hungarian People's Army. Tito looked to the West for assistance, and long-term economic relief was offered in 1949. It was delivered just in time to avert a devastating famine the following year.

The United States started sending weapons to Yugoslavia in 1951 but Tito refused to join NATO (he had also refused to join the Warsaw Pact). Instead he signed a tripartite pact with Greece and Turkey, which brought Yugoslavia closer to the West. Moscow's military threats eventually subsided when it became clear that the West was heavily committed to stopping the spread of communism as it deployed over 350,000 troops to stop the Chinese invasion of South Korea. Attitudes between Belgrade and Moscow thawed further after Stalin died in March 1953.

Connections with the West resulted in many changes across Yugoslavia in the 1950s, resulting in a unique form of Communism called Titoism. Certain restrictions were lifted as the state took an increasingly liberal view. The decentralised political system gave the six republics a degree of autonomy in the manner in which they implemented Belgrade's instructions. Meanwhile, diplomats avoided taking sides in the Cold War by refusing to get involved with their opposite numbers in Washington DC or Moscow.

Yugoslavia also developed a unique economic system, under which the government sponsored new industrial and infrastructure projects. Employee councils were allowed to control the means of production in their own factories to get optimum returns. They were then permitted to distribute the profits evenly across the workforce. The system was successful and both the nation's Gross Domestic Product and its exports increased at a steady rate. It meant that Yugoslavia was able to reduce its dependency on foreign aid, allowing it to maintain its independence.

Post-war Albania

Roosevelt, Stalin and Churchill never spoke about Albania's future during their series of wartime conferences. They also refused to recognise the Albanian government-in-exile after the country was liberated in November 1944. The communists took matters into their own hands by putting down a rebellion by the fascist National Front in December 1944 and seizing power for themselves. Political opponents and those who had collaborated with the occupying forces were then forced to flee the country or face imprisonment and execution.

The Anti-Fascist National Liberation Council took control of the country when the war ended. It meant that King Zog I had to stay in exile, while Enver Hoxha, a supporter of the Stalinist form of communism, was appointed prime minister. He would spend the post-war years strengthening his control of Albania by focusing on arresting war criminals and opponents to his policies rather than helping the tens of thousands of starving peasants.

The Albanians renounced their ambitions to annex Kosovo, beyond their north-eastern border, and Tito recognised their provisional government in return. However, Tirana had to accept Cham refugees exiled from Epirus, because Greece accused them of collaborating with the Nazis.

The state had taken control of all industries, trade and commerce as soon as the country was liberated. Property was confiscated from the political exiles and enemies of the state as well as from any Germans and Italians who had settled in the country before and during the war. Schools were set up to deal with illiteracy in an attempt to bring the country's education up to the same standard as its neighbours.

The Agrarian Reform Law of August 1945 appropriated privately-owned land; the result was that the peasants worked harder to improve its productivity because they benefited from their labours. Even so, Albania struggled to feed its people and both Yugoslavia and the United Nations Relief and Rehabilitation Administration (UNRRA) had to send aid to alleviate famine.

A new People's Assembly took control of Albania in December 1945. It declared the country was a People's Republic after abolishing the monarchy. Enver Hoxha's administration then introduced a constitution modelled on the Soviet system and the Stalin–style economy increased the state's control on industry, trade and property ownership.

All the members of the People's Assembly were from the communist Democratic Front and moderates soon found themselves in prison. Albania also became a dictatorship, with Hoxha acting as prime minister, foreign minister, defence minister and army commander. He was supported in the multiple roles by the Minister of Internal Affairs, Koçi Xoxe.

Albania may have been the poorest country in Europe but Tito still wanted it to be Yugoslavia's seventh republic. Greece also coveted part of its territory. Albania was separated from the rest of the Eastern Bloc by Yugoslavia, and a Treaty of Friendship, Cooperation and Mutual Aid was signed between the two countries in 1946. However, Tirana correctly believed that the treaty favoured its dominant neighbour.

Tito forced Tirana to get Belgrade's approval on all trade deals, ending the Albanian economy. He even interfered in Albanian attempts to improve relations with Bulgaria, looking to influence the situation across the Balkans. Tito even tried to get rid of Hoxha by convincing several members of the People's Assembly to back his plans. Hoxha retaliated to the interference in Albanian politics by having them arrested. Yugoslavia then accused Hoxha of ignoring the treaty and a huge loan was offered to turn the Albania people against their leader.

Nako Spiru, the head of Albania's Planning Commission, opposed the close ties with Yugoslavia and he supported Hoxha's decision to switch Albania's allegiance to Moscow in July 1947. Tito responded by helping

Koçi Xoxe and his *Sigaurimi*, Albania's security service, run a smear campaign. Spiru was soon found dead; the official line was that he had committed suicide.

The following spring, Xoxe accused Hoxha of orchestrating the decline in relations with Belgrade. The alignment with Moscow turned out to be a wise move after Yugoslavia was expelled from the Communist Information Bureau (Cominform) in June 1948. All treaties and agreements between Tirana and Belgrade ended the following month, leaving Albania isolated from the rest of the Eastern Bloc.

Hoxha instead joined the Council for Mutual Economic Assistance (Comecon) in February 1949, allowing Albania to trade with the rest of the Eastern Bloc. In return Moscow sent aid and technical and military advisers to help Albania's industries and armed forces.

As Albania improved its ties with the Soviet Union, the exiled members of the Legality Movement started working with the Western governments, looking to undermine the communist regime. Arguments with the National Front and the Independent Block may have hampered early negotiations, but the British Broadcasting Company (BBC) announced the formation of a National Committee in the United States in September 1949. The problem was, King Zog refused to support it.

Relations between Albania and the West had deteriorated after two British destroyers hit mines off its coast killing over forty sailors. Tirana claimed the ships were sailing in its waters but the International Court of Justice ruled against it.

The incident prompted Britain to consider how to overthrow Hoxha's communist regime and the Special Operations Executive sent a dozen trained exiles back into Albania in 1947. Their efforts failed to start a rebellion, so the United States joined in the attempt to topple the communist regime, with a view to sparking dissent behind the Iron Curtain. Their Secret Intelligence Service (SIS) parachuted royalist supporters into Albanian, hoping they could spark a local revolution. The long-term goal may have been to inspire a civil war, but they faced an uphill task because Albania was ruled by its Soviet-trained army and the *Sigaurimi*.

The Free Albania National Committee was formed in July 1949 and it began recruiting exiled members of the Albanian National Front and Legality Group. They were codenamed 'pixies' and trained on Malta for what the British called Operation Valuable and the Americans called Operation Fiend. The first operators landed in September 1949 but they were soon tracked down and either executed or forced to escape into Greece.

Later groups were intercepted not long after they arrived in Albania. The problem was that the British liaison officer working in Washington was Kim Philby and he was forwarding names and operational details to Moscow.

Over 300 agents had been killed and many more captured by the time the attempt to overthrow Albania was called off at the beginning of 1953. The survivors were put on trial in April 1954 and many were executed. The authorities also punished anyone believed to have assisted the agents. It brought the West's first attempt at paramilitary operations in the Eastern Bloc to a bloody end.

Although Albania was getting back on its feet with Soviet help, Hoxha blamed his Minister of the Interior for its problems and had him and another forty politicians executed in the summer of 1949. However, there were some who despised the connections with Moscow and they bombed the Soviet embassy in Tirana in March 1951. The secret police retaliated by stepping up their security measures while a law threatened the death penalty for treasonable crimes to anyone as young as 11 years old.

Albanian had been loosely following the Stalinist economic model since the end of the Second World War and a five-year plan launched in 1951 confirmed it would continue. Industry would expand, agricultural land would be collectivised and the nation's resources would be exploited. In the meantime, the Soviet Union provided loans until Albania had balanced its imports and exports. The drive to improve the economy resulted in improved living standards but little was known about the country because Albanians were banned from leaving and foreigners were not allowed to visit.

The Soviet Union and Albania remained close as Moscow poured millions of roubles into Tirana's economy. In return Soviet warships were allowed to deploy from its naval bases on the Adriatic coast while subsidising the building of a submarine base near the port of Vlorë.

The People's Republic of Bulgaria

The Fatherland Front had executed nearly one hundred of its opponents on 1 February 1945 to secure its grip on Bulgaria. Another 30,000 enemies of the state had been arrested and killed by the time the war came to an end on 8 May. The killing would continue in earnest, even after the war had ended.

The government-in-exile received little support from anyone living in Bulgaria because the new People's Court had declared that Prince Kyril and previous members of the government were guilty of war crimes.

The government-in-exile would disband at the end of the war and the ex-prime minister, Aleksandar Tsankov, went into exile in Argentina.

Bulgaria would be allowed to keep Southern Dobruja, along its northern border with Romania. However, it had to take in over 150,000 Bulgarians who were being thrown out of Western Thrace, along its southern border with Greece. Many of them had moved in during the Bulgarian occupation of the area and were escaping persecution.

Georgi Dimitrov returned to Bulgaria to replace Kimon Georgiev as head of the Fatherland Front in November 1945 after many years in exile. Bulgaria was declared a People's Republic in September 1946, the monarchy was abolished, and Tsar Simeon II was forced to leave the country. The communists dominated the next election, Vasil Kolarov became president, and Dimitrov was appointed the prime minister. The Workers Party was renamed the Communist Party and Bulgaria came under Moscow's control. Vâlko Chervenkov became both president and prime minister of Bulgaria when Dimitrov and Kolarov died in 1949 and 1950 respectively.

The Agrarian People's Union had originally refused to work with the Communists, so its leader Nikola Petkov had been arrested and executed. Both the Social Democrats and Agrarian People's Union ended up having to cooperate with the Fatherland Front. Bulgaria worked hard to copy the Soviet economic model, introducing industrialisation and collectivised farming. It also continued to execute thousands of enemies of the state, while tens of thousands more were imprisoned in forced labour camps.

Stalin wanted Pirin Macedonia, in south-west Bulgaria, to have cultural autonomy; anyone who opposed the plan was either imprisoned or deported to northern Serbia. Plans to merge the area with Vardar Macedonia, in south-east Yugoslavia, were abandoned after Stalin and Tito argued in 1948.

The Soviet occupation of Romania and the Communist takeover

King Michael and the political parties had deposed Antonescu and switched the country's allegiance from the Axis to the Allies when the Red Army approached Romania's border in August 1944. The Romanian armies then crossed Transylvania and joined the Red Army's fight against the Wehrmacht during the battles through Hungary, Czechoslovakia and Austria.

Romania may have helped the Allies during the final months of the war but Moscow had not forgotten that it had allowed Axis troops to deploy along its northern border before Operation Barbarossa. Over 150,000 Romanian troops had taken part in the German invasion of the Soviet Union and they had fought on the Eastern Front for over two years. They had also taken part in the Holocaust across the Ukraine. It meant that Roosevelt and Churchill had little choice but to acknowledge Moscow's interest in Romania at the Yalta Conference in February 1945.

King Michael was soon sidelined and Dr Petru Groza of the Ploughmen's Front was appointed prime minister of Romania in March 1945. Demonstrators took to the streets on 8 November 1945 and were confronted by the army and the police. Stalin eventually sent half a million Red Army soldiers to restore order, turning Romania into an occupied country. Large numbers of Soviet planes were also stationed on the country's airfields, giving Moscow air coverage of south-east Europe. Groza had appointed communists as his ministers and they set about introducing new laws without asking the monarch's consent. These included policies such as land reform and women's suffrage, which proved popular with the peasantry.

The nation's first post-war election was held in November 1946 but violence marred the campaign, while the Bloc of Democratic Parties easily won due to the fraudulent voting procedures. The communists then arrested and executed all those accused of collaborating with the Germans, including the nation's ex-prime minister Ion Antonescu. Total control was secured when they abolished the monarchy and forced King Michael to abdicate on 30 December 1947. Romania was then declared a People's Republic, while the Workers' Party was formed to run the country in February 1948. A constitution which formalised the new regime was announced two months later.

The communists dominated the Workers' Party as Romania took on a Soviet-inspired political direction. The outbreak of extremism, nepotism and backstabbing resulted in 200,000 members being thrown out of the party while thousands more were arrested. The banks and large businesses were nationalised as the government increased its control over the economy, forcing companies to export their surplus products to the Soviet Union at low prices.

Party leader Gheorghe Gheorghiu-Dej replaced Groza as Prime Minister in June and he made Romania switch from rural industries and agriculture to heavy industries and power stations. The change in direction resulted in higher wages, increased production and an end to rationing. He refused to follow the Soviet system of repression and as a result labour camps were closed and work on forced labour projects, such as the Danube–Black Sea Canal, was halted.

A Civil War across Greece

The Greek government and the Communist Party of Greece had signed the Treaty of Varkiza in February 1945. It meant that the communists' political arm, the EAM, would be allowed to operate, but members of the communists' military arm, the ELAS, had to hand over their weapons and demobilise. There would also be a general election and a referendum concerning the future of the monarchy.

A promise had been made to grant an amnesty for political offences, but the police falsely treated many cases as criminal activity and arrested 40,000; another 1,000 would be murdered. Some opponents of the government went into exile in Yugoslavia, while many others hid their weapons and waited for an opportunity to overthrow the government.

The Communist Party boycotted the March 1946 elections because Markos Vafiadis was busy organising a new military organisation called the Democratic Army. The United Nationalist Party won the election and an autumn vote resulted in King George returning to Greece. Even so, support for the communists continued to grow, with backing from the Yugoslav and Albanian governments. Reprisal actions against the communists increased and many innocent people were imprisoned or exiled, accused of helping them.

By 1947 the British were no longer able to send aid to Greece, and it would take the United States time to send any. The Democratic Army took advantage of the military's difficulties and started fighting for control of settlements, only for many to be killed in the battle for Konitsa in north-west Greece. The Communists resorted to forming a Provisional Democratic Government across the rural areas it controlled. It was soon banned and its members were arrested. Despite the setback, the Democratic Army stepped up its guerrilla activities and support for it continued to grow.

One disturbing aspect of the civil war was what happened to many Greek children. At the suggestion of Queen Frederica, around 25,000 were taken from their families and sent to camps away from the fighting. The government said it was to protect them from the fighting but others say it was because their parents were communist supporters. At the same time, it is believed that the communists were sending children to Eastern Bloc countries so they could be indoctrinated.

The Soviet Union split with Yugoslavia in the summer of 1948, leaving the communists confused over who they should support. Some chose to stand with the Party leader, Markos Vafiadis, who had aligned himself with

Yugoslavia's Tito, but the majority supported the Party secretary, Nikolaos Zachariadis. The Tito supporters were expelled from the Communist Party, so he retaliated by closing down the Democratic Army's training camps inside Yugoslavia.

General Alexander Papagos took command of the Hellenic Army and he used troops to intimidate the peasants to reduce their support for the communists. He then launched Operation Pyravlos (Rocket) in the summer of 1949, driving the Democratic Army from central Greece. Operation Pyrsos (Torch) finished communist resistance in Western Macedonia in August 1949. Over 100,000 communist guerrillas were imprisoned, exiled or executed, while a hardcore headed to Uzbekistan in the Soviet Union.

The communists would be accused of war crimes by the fascist regime which later ruled Greece. EAM was eventually recognised as a resistance movement in 1981 and only then were the ELAS fighters honoured for fighting the Axis forces.

Bulgaria, Romania and Albania came under Soviet control behind the Iron Curtain, while Greece joined NATO. However, Tito saw to it that Yugoslavia remained neutral during the Cold War years.

Chapter 11

Communist and Fascist Rule

March 1953 to December 1991

The death of Stalin in March 1953 changed the way the Balkan countries reacted to Soviet policies. Some governments worked closer with Moscow while others headed in their own direction. Many rejected the oppression forced upon them by communism, resulting in uprisings in Czechoslovakia and Hungary; Greece even turned to fascism, following a military takeover. Even so, Yugoslavia, Albania and Romania clung to their left-wing ideals and the personality cults surrounding their leaders.

Timeline

March 1953	Stalin dies
October 1956	An uprising in Hungary which results in the Red Army invading
March 1964	King Paul of Greece dies and is succeeded by King Constantine II
August 1965	Romania is renamed a Socialist Republic
April 1967	A military dictatorship seizes control of Greece
December 1967	King Constantine fails to launch a counter-coup in Greece
January 1968	An uprising in Czechoslovakia which results in the Red Army invading
November 1968	Greece's military junta introduces a new constitution
1971	The Croatian Spring uprising
June 1973	The Greek monarchy is abolished
November 1973	Martial law is re-established across Greece
February 1974	Yugoslavia announces a new constitution
November 1974	Greece becomes the Third Hellenic Republic

November 1976   Albania declares a new constitution

April 1985   First Secretary of the Albania Party of Labour, Enver
                Hoxha, dies

December 1989   Romanian President Nicolae Ceauşescu is executed

November 1998   The People's Socialist Republic of Albania comes to an
                end

The Socialist Federal Republic of Yugoslavia

The Yugoslavian Communist Party had changed its name to the League of
Communists in 1952, bringing together the six federal communist parties.
Tito then worked with his advisors to devise a new form of socialism to the
rest of Soviet-dominated Eastern Europe. Party and state bureaucracy were
cut back and power was decentralised, allowing each republic to administer
its area. Each place of work was permitted to organise a workers' council
which could set production to make the best use of its labour force and
facilities. Restrictions on civil rights were relaxed and the actions of the State
Security Administration were reduced. The media was still controlled but
exiled enemies of the state continued to be tracked down and assassinated.

Relations between Yugoslavia and the Soviet Union improved after First
Secretary Nikita Khrushchev's visit to Belgrade in May 1955. However,
arguments over how the economy should be run resulted in Tito supporting
calls for more decentralisation. Yugoslavia then made the most of having
borders with both the capitalist and communist parts of Europe by trading
with both.

The State Security Administration (*Uprava Državne Bezbednosti* or
UDBA) was accused of eavesdropping on Tito's conversations while the
Communist Party met on Brioni Island in 1966. The investigation that
followed resulted in the second resignation of Minister of the Interior
Aleksandar Ranković and many of his supporters. The organisation then
handed control of internal affairs to the republics, leaving the central office
to coordinate operations from Belgrade.

Despite economic success, the regional nationalist groups still wanted
independence. They were inspired when a student protest led to a national
uprising in Hungary in October 1956. The Red Army had to step in to help
the Hungarian Army and there had been over 22,000 civilian and 2,000
military casualties, most of them in Budapest, by the time the uprising was
crushed. Thousands of protesters were arrested while tens of thousands

more fled the country. Yugoslavia was blamed for encouraging the uprising and Moscow retaliated by instigating a new campaign against the Belgrade government. Tito refused to become involved with either the West or the East as the Cold War heated up; he focused on fostering diplomatic ties with Egypt and India instead.

Relations with Moscow deteriorated when the 'Prague Spring', a period of decentralising the economy, democratic reforms and the easing of personal restrictions, began in Czechoslovakia in January 1968. Half a million troops from five Warsaw Pact countries invaded Czechoslovakia the following August. The brutal repression resulted in over 600 civilian casualties followed by a mass exodus of 300,000 Czechoslovakians to the West.

Yugoslav students held their own demonstrations against economic reforms which threatened to increase unemployment. Tito gave in to their demands, only to order the UDBA to arrest the ring leaders over the months that followed. The League of Communists continued to stir up ethnic emotions as it called for more rights for the Croatians. It also demanded economic equality across Yugoslavia because it believed the Serbs were taking advantage of the other ethnic groups. Thousands of students wanted to make Croatian the official language of Croatia and demanded an equal spread of revenue in 1971. This movement was called the Croatian Spring, or *Maspok* (short for *Masovni Pokret* or Mass Movement). Moscow called on Belgrade to reassert itself, so Tito had the protesters arrested and then purged the Croatian Communist Party.

The 'Croatian Silence' followed as worried politicians shied away from upsetting the federal government. Tito gave the republics more power but he still had to remove Serb and Croat politicians who called for more. A new constitution in February 1974 eventually reset equality across Yugoslavia by giving the smaller republics and provinces extra powers to counter their larger neighbours. The Croatians and Albanians welcomed the changes but the Serbs were unhappy about losing their grip on the country. It seemed the only way to keep Yugoslavia together was to forcibly stop one area gaining an advantage over its neighbours.

A new constitution, which reduced the power of the central, federal government, was introduced in 1974. However, ethnic tensions increased following Tito's death in May 1980 and the constitution made it impossible to run the state effectively. Serbia may have had the most votes but the constitution allowed the other republics to form coalitions. So, they united, forming a majority to oppose Serbia.

Slobodan Milošević was anxious to restore Serbian sovereignty and he succeeded in reducing Slovenia's and Croatia's autonomy. However, the first major problem arose when the Albanian miners across Kosovo organised a strike in 1989. Demonstrations calling for a Kosovan republic resulted in the police force and army units being deployed to suppress them.

Arguments over the future of Yugoslavia dominated the Communist Congress in January 1990. The Serbian delegation wanted to impose a 'one person, one vote' system, because it would give them the majority. However, the Slovene and Croat delegations walked out of the Congress when their demands for increased autonomy were rejected.

The Yugoslav Communist Party disbanded in line with the fall of communism across Eastern Europe. Welcome though the return of democracy might have been, it led to a rise of nationalism as the republics prepared to hold their first multi-party elections for fifty years. Serbia was anxious to keep Yugoslavia together, while the rest of the republics were impatient to get their independence. A series of elections in 1990 would bring matters to a head.

Albania after Stalin

There were two weeks of national mourning across Albania following the death of Stalin in March 1953. However, Enver Hoxha and Mehmet Shehu dared not attend the funeral, fearing there would be a coup across Albania in their absence. Shehu was appointed Albania's prime minister the following year but both he and Hoxha opposed Soviet Premier Nikita Khrushchev's 'peaceful coexistence' and 'different roads to socialism' policies. They pursued Stalinism but they also worried that Moscow had resumed talking to Yugoslavia, raising concerns that Tito might resume his claim over Albania.

The authority of the exiled Free National Committee diminished when Albania joined the United Nations in 1955; it settled around 15,000 Albanian refugees across the United States. Albania may have also joined the Warsaw Treaty Organization, or Warsaw Pact, the same year but there were troubles ahead. Hoxha defended Stalin when Khrushchev denounced the crimes committed during his thirty-year rule of the Soviet Union. It left him paranoid, so he had pro-Soviet and pro-Yugoslav members expelled from the Communist Party; four senior members were executed.

Hoxha supported the People's Republic of China when it complained about the dismantling of Stalin's state. He called the rulers of the new

Soviet regime revisionists and traitors to Communism and preferred to do deals with Beijing rather than Moscow. Khrushchev retaliated by reducing grain imports when famine threatened Albania, in an attempt to undermine Hoxha's position.

A new Five-Year Plan, announced in February 1961, focused on improving Albania's industry. It contradicted the Soviet plan for the nation to maintain its agricultural economy. Moscow hit back by withdrawing aid and cutting diplomatic relations. Beijing stepped in but the Chinese equipment proved to be inferior and there were never enough advisors. Hoxha was forced to introduce austerity in 1962 as the country descended into a bureaucratic nightmare.

Mao Zedong's Cultural Revolution across China in 1966 convinced Hoxha to do the same, resulting in huge changes for the government, the economy and the armed forces. The revolution then shut down religion, because Hoxha believed it was dividing the people. Places of worship were shut and the teaching of religion was banned as Albania became the world's first atheist state.

Relations with Moscow deteriorated even more when the Warsaw Pact invaded Czechoslovakia in January 1968. Hoxha opposed the brutal oppression of the Prague Spring uprising and withdrew Albania from the Warsaw Pact in protest. Links between Tirana and Beijing cooled after 1970 because Albania started trading with the rest of the world and China started dealing with the United States. Mao died in 1976 and China's links with Albania ended when Tito visited Beijing the following year. Hoxha refused to deal with either the United States or the Soviet Union but an attempt to create a self-reliant economy ended when the economy collapsed.

Hoxha may have been old and frail but he sacked his military and economic advisors when they discussed replacing him. But he did recognise the end was approaching and stepped back from state affairs after announcing a new Stalinist constitution. It meant that Albania would continue to pursue communism, autarky and atheism.

One of Hoxha's legacies was the largest concentration of military bunkers in the world, brought about by paranoia. Tirana thought it was at war with Greece to the south and in conflict with Yugoslavia to the north, leaving Hoxha believing the country would soon have to save itself from either a North Atlantic Treaty Organization (NATO) invasion or a Warsaw Pact attack. Hoxha's response was to invest huge amounts of money the country did not have on fortifications.

Bunkers were built on every street corner and road junction and all places in between. Trained troops were detailed to man the command bunkers while the militia were trained from a young age to fight from the nearest bunker to their home. A quarter of the population was conscripted to serve in the armed forces at any one time but a lack of money meant that training was poor and supplies were lacking.

The military would have preferred to spend their money on maintaining a small and well-equipped professional army rather than a large militia, but Hoxha disagreed. He was adamant that the bunkers would save the country and Defence Minister General Beqir Balluku was executed after he criticised them in 1974. Other critics were arrested and Hoxha secured total control of Albania when a new constitution was introduced two years later. He also appointed himself commander of the Armed Forces and chairman of the Defence Council.

After twenty years of building, there were over 170,000 bunkers scattered across Albania, at an average density of fifteen per square mile. They may have represented a way of securing the country's future but they had placed a huge strain on the nation's economy when many people were homeless. The bunkers were never used and would be abandoned when communism collapsed in 1990.

Albania declared a new constitution in November 1976 and while the plan was to build a socialist society, some saw it as a return of capitalism. The country remained isolated and backward compared to the rest of Europe, but it continued to ban foreign investment or borrowing. The country had a very low standard of living but it also had very little foreign debt to interfere with its economy.

Ramiz Alia was chosen to succeed an ailing Hoxha in 1980. He tried to persuade Prime Minister Mehmet Shehu to stand down, criticising him for allowing his son to become engaged to the daughter of a former bourgeois family. Paranoia increased as politicians and civil servants were arrested and executed in 1981. Shehu allegedly committed suicide at the end of the year, though some thought he had been murdered. Hoxha would later accuse Shehu of being a spy who was planning to assassinate him.

Hoxha had been ill for some time when he died in April 1985. He left an Albania isolated from the rest of Europe. Thousands of bunkers covered the countryside, while the people were training to fight off imaginary invaders. His successor, Ramiz Alia, inherited a poor economy and an angry population. He was forced to introduce reforms and relax repression. He also opened diplomatic talks with West Germany and received aid in return.

Other communist governments came to an end in the wake of reforms across the Soviet Union but Alia increased reforms to prevent an uprising. He cracked down even more after the arrest and execution of Romanian President Nicolae Ceaușescu in December 1989. There would be no open government or economic reform (*glasnost* or *perestroika*) in Albania.

Albania eventually signed the Helsinki Accords, fifteen years after the rest of the world, bringing the nation up to date on political, economic and human rights issues. Relations with the country's neighbours slowly improved, and demonstrations in December 1990 led to Alia agreeing to implement more changes. However, the coalition government still collapsed in December 1991 and the Democratic Party of Albania won the election the following spring by promising reforms to ease the nation into capitalism. However, it failed to live up to expectations and was forced to rig the June 1996 election to remain in power.

Alia and other senior party officials were eventually imprisoned for abusing power and stealing public money. The country's economy collapsed in 1997 under the weight of a number of corrupt financial pyramid schemes, and the military was too corrupt to stop an uprising. A constitution was approved and the country voted its first democratic government into power for seventy years. The People's Socialist Republic finally came to an end in November 1998 when a new constitution was implemented.

Communist Bulgaria

Vâlko Chervenkov had been appointed prime minister of Bulgaria in 1950 and while he expanded industry, he also brought Bulgaria's economic activity under government control. Agriculture was collectivised and productivity increased, but there were still food shortages and thousands died when the crops failed.

Chervenkov also established state healthcare and education systems, but the labour employed on building projects was provided by those arrested for opposing the state. Despite the improvements, Chervenkov's support waned after Stalin died in 1953 and he was replaced when Bulgaria denounced Stalinism in 1956. Anton Yugov was appointed Prime Minister, Todor Zhivkov became the leader of the Bulgarian Communist Party, and they introduced reform and a liberal approach in line with the new Soviet leader, Nikita Khrushchev. The recent purges and executions were denounced and Chervenkov was suspended from the Communist Party.

The Bulgarian government found itself having to reassert itself in the wake of protests in Poland and the Hungarian revolution in 1956. Bulgaria had borrowed heavily from Western countries in the 1950s to keep its economy afloat. By 1960 it was broke and Sofia was forced to sell over one hundred tons of gold and silver to Moscow to reduce the debt to a manageable amount. Todor Zhivkov took over as Prime Minister and Party Secretary when Anton Yugov retired in 1962 and he introduced reforms to improve the economy. Companies and farmers were allowed to increase production above government quotas, so the surplus could be sold across the Eastern Bloc. However, there was little planning, which resulted in surpluses of some products and shortages of others.

The Bulgarian People's Army was a member of the Warsaw Pact and most of its equipment was supplied by the Soviet Union. Troops would provide support and assistance to communist countries, such as North Korea and the Viet Cong, and it would take part in several conflicts around the world in the 1960s. Sofia also supported the Warsaw Pact's invasion of Czechoslovakia during the Prague Spring of January 1968. Over 2,000 Bulgarian troops would cross the border, but they did not take an active part in putting down the uprising.

Zhivkov even decided to act against Greece in 1971, to undermine the right-wing military junta. The plan to carry out an arson attack against the main Greek Orthodox church in Constantinople was concocted with a view to blaming the Turkish Muslims. Operation Cross had a good chance of destabilising NATO's Balkan ally but the plan was shelved.

Stanko Todorov was appointed Prime Minister in 1917 as Bulgaria starting working with a new constitution. Sofia may have signed the Helsinki Accords in 1975, but only Christians were afforded the human rights and freedoms prescribed under its articles. Bulgaria usually stayed out of the press but it came to the world's attention when its secret service agents assassinated the writer Georgi Markov in 1978. Markov had defected to the West in 1969 and became a marked man after making critical radio broadcasts about the Bulgarian regime. He was killed by ricin poison jabbed into his leg with an umbrella on the streets of London.

Romania under Communism

President Gheorghe Gheorghiu-Dej handed control of the Romanian Worker's Party to Gheorghe Apostol in 1954, only to take it back the following year. He then negotiated Romania's membership of both the

United Nations and the Warsaw Treaty Organization (Warsaw Pact). While Bucharest followed Moscow's example in many matters, it would not allow the Red Army to practice manoeuvres on its soil. It hardly ever sent troops to take part in exercises in other countries either.

Romanian students discussed revolutionary plans after Poland stood up to Moscow's demands in June 1956. They became even more agitated when revolution threatened across Hungary in October 1956. The Romanian regime countered by harassing the dissidents and hundreds were exiled, imprisoned or suspended from their courses. As the Red Army deployed extra troops along the Hungarian border, Romania promised the Hungarian Prime Minister and revolution leader Imre Nagy safe passage. However, the Soviets were allowed to arrest and interrogate him when they launched Operation Whirlwind. Nagy was tried and executed in secret.

Gheorghiu-Dej set about securing his control of Romania by sacking the Stalinists from his government. He then removed all those who disapproved of his leadership from the Communist Party. The level of surveillance carried out by the Romanian secret police (*Securitate*) was increased, as did the number of arrests, with members of the intelligentsia being targeted. Many more prisons were opened, as were the number of construction projects being built by forced labour. Work restarted on the canal connecting the Danube to the Black Sea.

Gheorghiu-Dej's government may have implemented economic policies to improve life for many but it also forcibly relocated peasants from isolated rural areas onto collective farms. Tens of thousands would die from food shortages and anyone who complained faced the wrath of the Securitate or the army.

Gheorghiu-Dej died in March 1965 and Chivu Stoica took his place as President. Nicolae Ceaușescu was appointed First Secretary of the Workers' Party. They would rename the country the Socialist Republic of Romania in August. Ceaușescu proved to be popular, helped by the fact that he kept the economy buoyant by negotiating with Western countries, to Moscow's disapproval. He also criticised the Soviet invasion of Czechoslovakia in August 1968. The government's main concern was Romania's low birth rate. It introduced several laws to spark a baby boom, including the banning of contraception and abortions. Legislation favoured large families, while childless couples faced higher taxation. The new laws were successful in creating the desired population increase but many parents were unable to feed their expanding families. Many women died after seeking an illegal abortion, while desperate mothers handed their children to state orphanages in the hope they would get adopted.

Romania joined the International Monetary Fund and the World Bank in 1972 because it planned to become more integrated into world economics. Visits to North Korea and China also inspired Ceauşescu to start a cultural revolution, which involved investing heavily in new industries and infrastructure. An earthquake damaged a large area of Bucharest in 1977 and the widespread demolition which followed presented an opportunity to accelerate the city-centre regeneration programme. Romania also introduced a nationwide programme of urban planning, called Systematization, which involved bulldozing many old buildings to make way for modern apartment blocks. Ceauşescu also wanted a huge palace and government district, which involved the demolition of a large medieval area in central Bucharest.

The new housing and updated cultural buildings may have increased conditions for many Romanians, but they still faced the lowest living standards in Europe. Production also increased in line with industrialisation but so did the amount of pollution, and people's health suffered as a result.

One of Ceauşescu's targets was to reduce the nation's debt to Western countries, so rationing was introduced while surplus products were sold abroad in return for hard cash. Romania finished paying off its overseas debts early, in March 1989, but the harsh austerity measures had required the Securitate to intensify its grip on society.

An open system of government (*Glasnost*) and a reformed economic system (*Perestroika*) was introduced by Mikhail Gorbachev in the Soviet Union in 1988 but Romania remained a communist regime. Ceauşescu was re-elected secretary general of the Communist Party in November 1989 but trouble was brewing because of his hard-line stance. On 16 December 1989 an impromptu protest in Timişoara, following Bishop László Papp's attempt to evict pastor László Tőkés from his apartment for daring to criticise the regime, escalated into a major riot aimed at the Romanian Communist Party. Dozens were killed or injured in the fighting over the days that followed and President Ceauşescu blamed foreign interference for the violence during a televised speech on 20 December.

The state imposed a curfew but news of the Timişoara protest led to more spontaneous riots across Romania. Ceauşescu decided to give a public speech to the crowds gathering outside the Central Committee Building in Bucharest, only to be shocked when they heckled and booed. Widespread riots followed as the army deployed to help the police and the Securitate tackle the protesters. Around 1,100 civilians would be killed as the rioting spread across the country.

Minister of Defence General Vasile Milea was reported to have taken his own life on 22 December, but many thought he had been murdered by the state (a later investigation suggested that he had tried to injure himself so he could step down from his post but the wound was fatal). Members of the armed forces responded to the news by joining the rioters and the country descended into chaos.

The protesters surrounded the Central Committee Building, nearly seizing Ceaușescu and his wife before a helicopter extracted them from the building's roof. The Ceaușescus intended destination was their home in Snagov, but the helicopter diverted to Târgoviște, where it was grounded by armed troops. Police arrested the pair and handed them over to the army. Nicolae and Elena Ceaușescu were court-martialled and executed by firing squad on 25 December 1989. Their deaths brought an end to forty-three years of communist rule across Romania.

Greece's Military Dictatorship

The civil war had divided Greece into left-wing and right-wing camps, resulting in a conflict which had killed thousands and undermined the economy, creating tremendous hardship for many. Thousands were held in prisons or stuck on deserted Aegean islands, while many more had headed abroad looking for a safe, new life.

Greece had been a member of NATO since 1952 and preparations had been put in place to defend the country if the Warsaw Pact looked like it was going to invade. The Allies organised Operation Gladio to support special forces teams (called Mountain Raiding Companies) which would monitor the political situation across Greece. However, problems arose when an investigation into the assassination of the Union Democratic Left's leader, Gregorios Lambrakis, discovered right-wing connections with the police and the army. The prime minister and head of the National Radical Union, Konstantinos Karamanlis, was implicated and he was forced to resign.

The new Centre Union may have helped the United Democratic Left to victory during the 1963 election but now there were concerns it was involved with the Greek communists. So Prime Minister Papandreou planned to block their influence by announcing the popular policies he planned to implement and then resigned. He won a majority in a second election and he then appointed King Paul's favourites to his cabinet to secure the Centre Union's position.

Unfortunately Paul died in March 1964 and Papandreou was soon at odds with his 23-year-old son King Constantine II. The problem increased when a group of junior officers, calling themselves ASPIDA (an acronym for 'Officers Save Fatherland Ideals Democracy Meritocracy' and also the Greek word for 'Shield'), exposed the nepotism used by the Sacred Bond of Hellenic Officers, the army's old guard. Petros Garoufalias was harangued out of the post of Minister of Defence while investigating the scandal. Constantine then refused to let Georgios Papandreou take over the office because his son, Andreas Papandreou, was implicated in the scandal. Papandreou retaliated by resigning with the rallying call 'the King reigns but the people rule'. Constantine was then forced to choose several prime ministers in quick succession but they all failed to deal with the public's discontent.

The National Radical Union were worried that the left-wing Centre Union Party would spark a constitutional crisis if it won the May 1967 elections. So right-wing army officers sent tanks onto the streets of Athens on 21 April as their men arrested key people including Georgios and Andreas Papandreou. A military dictatorship, headed by Brigadier General Stylianos Pattakos and Colonels Nikolaos Makarezos and Georgios Papadopoulos, then seized control of the country. Over 10,000 opponents of the regime were arrested in a few days, many others would be exiled in the weeks that followed.

King Constantine refused to oppose the generals and instead swore them in. The election was cancelled, the constitution was abolished and Konstantinos Kollias was appointed Greece's new prime minister. The military junta called themselves the 'Revolution of 21 April' and they started ruling the country by decree.

King Constantine had reluctantly agreed to the Colonels' Regime undemocratic style of government and he was soon plotting a counter-coup to get rid of them with his loyal generals. Constantine and Kollias headed to the north of the country on 13 December 1967 looking to take control of Thessaloniki, gain international support and force the junta to stand down. The Air Force and Navy mobilised in the support of the king but junior army officers arrested their senior officers. Troops then tried to intercept the King, only he fled to Rome with his family and Kollias.

Major General Georgios Zoitakis was appointed Regent and the new constitution turned Greece into a police state with little regard for human rights. The junta controlled the media, used propaganda to promote ideas and blamed the communists for the country's misfortunes. Hundreds of opponents were arrested and tortured before they were imprisoned or exiled to one of the Aegean islands. The military police stopped demonstrations, often using violence, while the security police carried out surveillance of all aspects of life, even banning photography in public locations.

The United States continued to support Greece because it gave NATO a useful base in the Eastern Mediterranean. Generous aid stimulated the Greek economy, reduced unemployment and kept inflation low. But the amount of spending also resulted in a number of high-profile financial scandals.

Greece may have been experiencing an economic turnaround but many wanted democracy to return and an end to the human rights abuses.

A failed attempt to assassinate Georgios Papadopoulos in August 1968 resulted in the arrest, torture and imprisonment of the politician Alexandros Panagoulis. The protests against the military junta continued, with huge crowds turning out to demonstrate at the funeral of Georgios Papandreou in November 1968. Even larger crowds would turn out in September 1972 for the funeral of the author Giorgos Seferis, a Nobel Prize recipient who had spent two years in prison for opposing the regime.

The junta introduced a new constitution in November 1968, which stripped the monarchy of its powers. Georgios Papadopoulos appointed himself Regent and then declared that King Constantine was 'a collaborator with foreign forces and murderers' accusing him of wanting to rule Greece's politics. The junta continued to persecute anyone accused of opposing their rule, while others headed into exile so they could continue their protests. Students often protested against the regime and Kostas Georgakis focused the world's attention on human rights' abuses across Greece when he set himself on fire in Genoa in September 1970. Even foreign visitors, such as the German journalist Günter Wallraff, were imprisoned if they joined the demonstrations.

The junta divided into groups with different agendas as the months passed and they began arguing over how Greece should be run. Georgios Papadopoulos implemented reforms to stop the hard-line colonels turning the country into an authoritarian regime. He also tried forming Advisory Councils but had to start introducing democratic changes when the idea failed.

There were protests, although negotiations stopped the largest one at Athens law school in February 1973. Then in May, Commander Nikolaos Pappas heard that naval officers had been arrested for speaking out about the junta while on a NATO exercise. So he refused to sail his ship, the HNS

Velos, back to its home port, to raise awareness of the situation in Greece. A compromise was eventually agreed, under which the officers stayed on board while the crew were allowed to return to Greece to discuss the situation.

Papadopoulos eventually abolished the monarchy in June 1973, even banning King Constantine from returning to Greece. He then declared himself president of a new republic after winning a rigged referendum. He sacked the junta members from his cabinet and appointed Spyros Markezinis as his prime minister.

Papadopoulos ended martial law and released political prisoners, but the regime was soon struggling with the imposition of democracy. Many civilians rebelled because they believed that the country was just being taken over by a different form of dictatorship. Army officers were particularly aggrieved because their commanders were being sacked and they were soon planning how to seize back control.

Tanks and troops had to be deployed on the streets to deal with a student strike at the Athens Polytechnic in November 1973. Brigadier Dimitrios Ioannidis used the event as an excuse to deploy the military police a few days later. An election was cancelled and martial law was reinstated, while a puppet government took control of Greece. General Phaedon Gizikis and Adamantios Androutsopoulos replaced Papadopoulos and Markezinis and they immediately reversed the transition to democracy. It meant that arrests, torture, expulsions and censorship returned.

General Dimitrios Ioannides was determined to take control of Cyprus after its president, Archbishop Makarios III, expelled all Greek officers. The island was secured at the third attempt, on 5 July 1974, but Turkey struck back with Operation Atilla a few days later. The fighting that followed resulted in thousands killed and hundreds of thousands of Greek-Cypriots fleeing Cyprus.

The military junta imploded as a result of the disaster and President Phaedon Gizikis summoned politicians and heads of the armed forces to discuss how to avoid war with Turkey. Celebrations followed the announcement that Greece would once more be allowed to elect a government. There were even more celebrations when Gizikis convinced Konstantinos Karamanlis to return from exile.

Karamanlis' government released political prisoners and sacked anyone connected to the dictatorship. The Communist Party was allowed to enter politics again, after nearly thirty years in the political wilderness, but Karamanlis' New Democracy Party won the November 1974 election.

A referendum voted in favour of the Third Hellenic Republic, resulting in the appointment of President Konstantinos Tsatsos and a new constitution.

The new government had the junta members arrested and put on trial in Korydallos Prison in the summer of 1975. Papadopoulos, Pattakos, Makarezos and Ioannidis were found guilty of treason and insurrection but their death sentences were commuted to life imprisonment. Trials of those responsible for putting down the Athens Polytechnic uprising and the regime's torturers followed.

The transition to democracy was called the *Metapolitefsi* and the Greeks enjoyed a return of civil liberties. However, the authorities soon became mired in allegations of corruption and nepotism and the nation's economy became overwhelmed with public debt. One of Karamanlis' last acts would be to take Greece into the European Union, because Andreas Papandreou's Panhellenic Socialist Movement (PASOK) won the October 1981 election.

The division of Yugoslavia into ethnic states following the Balkans conflict.

Chapter 12

The Balkans Conflict

June 1991 to June 1999

Background

The Socialist Federal Republic of Yugoslavia had been established in 1945 and nationalism had been suppressed until President Josip Broz Tito died in 1980. The end of the strict regime allowed the republics to start arguing again and while Serbia wanted to take control, Croatia and Slovenia were looking for their independence. Slobodan Milošević was accused of wanting an independent state of Serbia which would annex the parts of Croatia and Bosnia where there was a Serb majority.

Yugoslavia's single political party system was abolished in January 1990, bringing an end to forty-five years of Communist rule. The Socialist Party of Serbia won the elections in four out of the eight areas, allowing Milošević to dominate Yugoslav politics. It resulted in the Slovene and Croatian delegates walking out of the parliament after he blocked their proposals. Both Slovenia and Croatia defiantly declared their independence but Prime Minister Ante Marković declared it was illegal to do so and instructed the Yugoslav Army to stop them taking steps towards autonomy.

Timeline of the Balkans Conflict

Summer 1990	The Log Revolution, followed by Croatia declaring independence
Summer 1991	The Ten-Day War, followed by Slovenia declaring independence
March 1991	Croatian War of Independence begins
March 1992	Bosnia-Herzegovina declares independence
February 1992	Bosnian Serbs form the *Republika Srpska*
February 1992	Deployment of a multi-national peacekeeping force

April 1992	Start of the Bosnian War
October 1993	Conflict between the Bosniaks and Croats begins
November 1994	International Criminal Tribunal makes its first indictment
November 1995	Croatia gains its independence
November 1995	The Dayton Agreement ends the Bosnian War
February 1996	The Kosovan Liberation Army attacks government targets
May 1999	Belgrade rejects a peace deal so NATO bombs Serb targets

April 1992   Start of the Bosnian War

April 1992   Serbia and Montenegro form a new federation

October 1993   Conflict between the Bosniaks and Croats begins

November 1994   International Criminal Tribunal makes its first indictment

November 1995   Croatia gains its independence

November 1995   The Dayton Agreement ends the Bosnian War

February 1996   The Kosovan Liberation Army attacks government targets

May 1999   Belgrade rejects a peace deal so NATO bombs Serb targets

The Log Revolution in Croatia (1990)

The Croatian Democratic Union won the April 1990 election after demanding an independent Croatia, and Franjo Tuđman was appointed the first President of Croatia. There was discrimination against the Serbs, including the sacking of civil servants from their government posts. The Serbs reacted angrily to the pro-Croat policies, blockading roads across central Croatia in the summer of 1990 in what became known as the Log Revolution.

The predominantly Serb area of Kninska Krajina declared itself an autonomous oblast. It then added extra areas before changing its name to the *Krajina Autonomous Oblast* (SAO Krajina). The objective was to unify with neighbouring Serbia but there were regular confrontations between Serb paramilitaries and the Croatian police.

The Ten-Day War in Slovenia (1991)

Slovenia introduced parliamentary reforms in September 1989 and the Democratic Opposition of Slovenia won the election the following April. There was an overwhelming call for independence during the December referendum and Slovenia left the Socialist Federal Republic of Yugoslavia on 25 June 1991. The Federal government responded by instructing the Yugoslav Army to secure the border. There were minor confrontations with the Slovenian police and territorial soldiers in what became known as the 'Ten-Day War'. The Brioni Agreement postponed the secession for three months, giving the Yugoslav Army time to withdraw its units from Slovenia.

The Croatian War of Independence (1991–5)

A referendum in May 1991 resulted in two things: SAO Krajina confirmed it would join Serbia; and the Croatians voted in favour of independence. Croatia declared it would separate from Yugoslavia on 25 June and the Serbs declared Serb-only zones. The Brioni Agreement arranged for a three-month delay, to give the Croats time to organise their departure, but there were skirmishes as 70,000 soldiers deployed to the area.

The Yugoslav Army was supposed to keep the peace but the Serb officers opposed the independence process. They disarmed the Croatian territorial units while handing out weapons to the Serb rebels, leading to an increase in violence. The United Nations eventually imposed an arms embargo on Yugoslavia in September but illegal weapons and ammunition continued to pour into the area.

Around 1,800 Croatian fighters deployed to oppose the Yugoslav Army's deployment across north-east Croatia in August 1991. Planes and artillery targeted Vukovar on the River Danube but the Croats refused to withdraw, while fighting around Dubrovnik, on the Adriatic coast, intensified in October.

Serb soldiers wreaked their revenge when the Croats defending Vukovar ran out of ammunition on 18 November. Soldiers and civilians alike were taken prisoner, taken to Ovčara Farm and executed. The European Community Monitor Mission and the International Red Cross Committee had agreed that the 300 patients in Vukovar hospital would be evacuated but the Yugoslav soldiers handed them over to Serbian troops and paramilitaries. They too were executed at Ovčara Farm, in just one of many massacres across Croatia.

Reports of fighting, intimidation and massacres sent tens of thousands fleeing from the war zones, creating a humanitarian crisis. The rest of Europe was slow to react to the calamity, resulting in parts of Croatia being overwhelmed by the masses of refugees.

Around 10,000 people had been killed and hundreds of thousands more had been forced to flee before the UN had managed to establish four protected areas for the Serbs across the Krajina Republic in January 1992. The Sarajevo Plan (or Vance Plan, named after US Secretary of State Cyrus Vance) kept the ground forces at a safe distance, but artillery and warplanes were still operating. The Croatians maintained their claim over the protected areas and continued to attack them until Operations Flash and Storm ended the fighting in 1995.

The United Nations Transitional Administration for Eastern Slavonia took control of the rest of the Krajina Republic in January 1996. Its 5,000 military and civilian staff would monitor the demilitarisation of the area before it was handed back to Croatia, under the 1998 Erdut Agreement.

The Bosnian War (1992-5)

Bosnia and Herzegovina held an independence referendum at the beginning of 1992. The Yugoslav army may have interfered in the voting process and the Serbs may have boycotted the vote but the Muslim Bosniaks still voted for independence. The new state was recognised by the European Union but the Bosnian Serbs objected and they established the *Republika Srpska*. The Serbs then supplied their compatriots while the Croatians supported the Bosniaks as both looked to divide the new state and seize territory. The United Nations ruled that Bosnia and Herzegovina must be allowed to remain independent, but the Serbs continued to contest the decision.

Radovan Karadžić promised that the Serbs would maintain their independence, as they began murdering or driving Bosniaks from the areas they coveted. The fighting included prolonged sieges of Sarajevo, Srebrenica and Goražde in the south-east of the country, as well as massacres in several smaller towns.

The announcement of the UN Security Council's Resolution 743 resulted in a multinational peacekeeping force being deployed to the Balkans in February 1992 to curb the violence. The United Nations Protection Force (UNPROFOR) was divided into three forces and they were given different responsibilities across Croatia, Bosnia and Herzegovina and Macedonia. The hardest task was making sure regular ground and air aid convoys could reach Sarajevo in Bosnia and Herzegovina safely, starting in June. Only then could it start escorting relief convoys to the many remote, rural settlements.

It took UNPROFOR until the spring of 1993 to establish three safe areas in Croatia under the UN's Confidence Restoration Operation or UNCRO. Each area used a protected boundary and restricted access points, referred to as pink zones, to prevent violent confrontations. After twelve months of peace talks it was possible to implement a weapons amnesty to further reduce the chance of armed incidents. Nearly 40,000 personnel from forty-two countries would serve with UNPROFOR over the course of three years.

During the peace talks, the Serbs used violence and rumours to force over 100,000 Croats to leave their area. The flood of refugees would overwhelm UNPROFOR and the Canadian Operational Force had to open Sarajevo airport. Transport aircraft started delivering supplies in July 1992. The peacekeepers managed to distribute humanitarian aid across Bosnia and Herzegovina but Serb paramilitaries often disrupted their efforts during the winter months causing extra hardship for tens of thousands of civilians.

The alliance between the Bosniaks and Croats ended because they engaged in separate negotiations. Clashes between the Army of the Republic of Bosnia and Herzegovina and the Croatian Defence Council followed in October 1992. A UN Security Council resolution had to ban unauthorised military flights over Bosnia, while NATO warplanes monitored the airspace under Operation Sky Monitor.

Srebrenica had been declared a 'Safe Area' but that did not stop Serb paramilitary units driving the Croats out of it in March 1993. Croat paramilitaries did the same to Serb and Bosniak civilians in other areas as the violence increased. Each side pursued ethnic cleansing policies as their ground troops attacked aid convoys and massacred civilians while their warplanes dropped bombs on villages.

An extra 7,500 ground troops were added to the UNPROFOR, but they were only permitted to act in self-defence, meaning they could only react to attacks on civilians and air convoys. NATO air support also had to be stepped up so that a new resolution to ban all unauthorised flights could be implemented.

In September 1993, the Croatian government insisted that the UNPROFOR left or implemented the Security Council resolutions and protected the Safe Areas properly. They did not get a satisfactory reply, bringing the year-long truce between the Serbs and Croats to an end. Fighting continued throughout the winter and outside interference increased the violence. Croat army units were accused of removing their identification as they fought alongside the Bosnian Croats. Meanwhile the Bosnian Serbs continued to shell Sarajevo, hoping they could force the Bosniaks to leave. Matters came to a head when a mortar shell hit one of the busy markets causing around 250 civilian casualties on 5 February 1994. The Bosnian Serbs were told to withdraw or surrender all their guns and mortars. They had met the terms of the ultimatum by the time the Washington Agreement arranged a ceasefire between the Croats and Serbs at the end of the month. The Agreement also resulted in the creation of the Federation of Bosnia and Herzegovina.

Protection Force units moved into the area to enforce the ceasefire and an extra 10,000 reinforcements had to be deployed to monitor it. The Croats and Serbs may have agreed to a ceasefire but the Bosnia Serbs had not and they continued to attack the peacekeepers and the safe areas. The UN Security Council's complaints were ignored, so NATO planes started bombing Bosnian Serb positions on 10 April. The Bosnian Serbs only ceased fire after an ultimatum threatening to step up the air attacks was issued on 24 April.

No less than five strategies for peace were turned down before the Serb, Croat and Bosnian representatives agreed to the sixth in July 1994. Unfortunately the Bosnian Serbs rejected the plan, forcing the Serbian government to cut relations with them. As a result, the number of attacks against UNPROFOR ground troops increased and NATO pilots encountered heavier anti-aircraft fire.

The Security Council accepted the peace plan laid down in Resolution 942 on 23 September 1994. It also resolved to stop supplies and money being sent to the Bosnian Serbs, to reduce their ability to fight. However, the Bosnian Muslims took matters into their own hands before anything could be done, by trying to break the siege. The increase in fighting led to more refugees fleeing the area, as the Bosnian Serbs began shelling and bombing the Bihać Safe Area.

NATO planes struck back at targets around the Udbina airstrip, but the Bosnian Serbs refused to discuss a cease fire. Instead they struck back by taking UN peacekeepers hostage and attacking aid convoys so that they could take the supplies themselves.

Croat forces captured over 200 square miles of the territory of SAO Krajina in May 1995. The three-day attack, codenamed Operation Flash, was supported by NATO aircraft. The Army of Republika Srpska then seized weapons from a UN arms dump after the Army of the Republic of Bosnia and Herzegovina attacked Sarajevo in May 1995. NATO planes attacked their positions around the city of Pale, so they retaliated against a UN post on the River Vrbanja. The Bosnians brought the air attacks to an end by taking 400 peacekeepers hostage and used them as human shields.

Massacres had been commonplace during the Balkans' conflicts but news of the one at Srebrenica in July 1995 shocked the world. The town had been designated a Bosniak safe zone but the United Nations Protection Force (UNPROFOR) failed to stop Bosnian Serb soldiers capturing the town. Bosnia and Herzegovinian soldiers tried to escort the civilians to safety but some were ambushed while others were tricked into surrendering. Around 8,000 Bosniak men and boys were murdered while many more women were raped or sexually abused.

A much larger Croatian attack (the largest land battle since the Second World War), codenamed Operation Storm, was launched against Republika Srpska in August 1995. This time 4,000 square miles were captured; 175,000 Serb civilians fled the fighting. NATO and UNPROFOR then planned to launch Operation Deliberate Force on 30 August 1995. But the preliminary air attacks alerted the Bosnian Serbs. They overwhelmed peacekeepers and again deployed them as human shields, so the air strikes were called off and the offensive was cancelled.

A third Croatian attack, named Operation Maestral II, seized key towns along the south-west border of Republika Srpska the following month, creating a buffer zone. The Bosnian and Herzegovinian armed forces countered with Operation Sana along Republika Srpska's north-west border. The final Croatian attack, Operation Southern Move, seized Manjača Mountain, overlooking Banja Luka, the Bosnian Serb capital. It also captured Republika Srpska's only power station, forcing the Bosnian Serbs to the negotiating table.

Peace Enforcement and Peace Keeping

The United Nations Security Council relied on Chapter VII of its charter to guide its policies during the Balkans conflict. Military units were given two types of operations to complete: peace enforcement and peacekeeping. They each had different objectives, which involved different problems to solve.

Once a commitment to peace had been agreed by the politicians, heavily armed troops had to move into an area to enforce the peace. This involved manning roadblocks and patrolling areas, to stop armed clashes and tit-for-tit ethnic violence. This allowed ceasefires to be arranged while aid convoys could be escorted into an area to help the refugees.

The objective once the fighting had stopped was to stop it flaring up again; a role referred to as peacekeeping. Troops had to keep the opposing factions apart to protect the civilian enclaves they were guarding. It would also hold weapons amnesties. The UN peacekeepers could then prepare the area for elections and start handing over security duties to the local emergency services to help return life to normal. The soldiers were often referred to as the Blue Helmets or Blue Berets because of their headgear.

The problem was, the people often thought the peace enforcers would be unable to stop the violence, so they hid their weapons in case it flared up. If the peace endured, many sold their weapons on the black market to raise money to feed their families. It resulted in large amounts of arms and ammunition ending up in the wrong hands. Criminals have since been selling them on to the highest bidder and some have found their way into the hands of terrorists and been used in recent incidents across Europe.

The Dayton Agreement

Plans to get the three presidents to meet in the United States, away from the media spotlight, had first been suggested in 1992. However, nothing was organised until after the Croatian Operation Storm and NATO's Operation Deliberate Force in August 1995. Presidents Slobodan Milošević of Serbia, Franjo Tuđman of Croatia and Alija Izetbegović of Bosnia and Herzegovina eventually gathered at Dayton, Ohio, in November 1995.

They came to an agreement which was signed in Paris the following month. It brought to an end the bloodiest conflict in Europe since the Second World War, one in which around 100,000 people, mostly civilians, had died; another two million had been forced to leave their homes.

The post-Dayton Peace Keeping Forces

The signing of the Dayton Agreement by the presidents of Bosnia, Croatia, and Serbia in December 1995 called for an end to the fighting. The agreement divided Bosnia into the Federation of Bosnia-Herzegovina and the Republika Srpska. Unfortunately, the complicated form of government would highlight the ethnic issues rather than giving them shared goals. It would need a much heavier military presence to keep the General Framework Agreement for Peace in place while elections were arranged.

Security Council Resolution 1031 called for the Implementation Force (IFOR) to take over from the Protection Force. Over 55,000 NATO soldiers from thirty-two countries moved in and it would be the first time that American and Russian troops had served alongside each other since the Second World War. Joint Force Commander, United States Admiral

Leighton Smith Jr., was given responsibility for Operation Joint Endeavour. His objectives were to use military force to restore the peace, assist civil projects implemented to maintain the peace, and support the new Bosnian government. British officer Lieutenant General Michael Walker took command of the Allied Rapid Reaction Corps; its three multinational divisions were responsible for carrying out the ground element of the operation, Operation Firm Endeavour.

The British controlled the north-west part of Bosnia-Herzegovina, from Banja Luka, while the Americans ran the north-east area from Tuzla. The French controlled operations in the south from Mostar, while a support group organised the distribution of supplies and logistics from Pécs in south-west Hungary. Warships were deployed in the Adriatic Sea in a support role while warplanes would fly over 250 missions a week over the area.

As soon as the Dayton Agreement had been implemented, Security Council Resolution 1088 called for the military presence across Bosnia and Herzegovina to be scaled down. The Stabilisation Force (SFOR) took over peace enforcement duties in December 1996; its size would vary according to the threat. Again, the multinational force divided Bosnia-Herzegovina between three ground forces and they continued to be based at Banja Luka, Tuzla and Mostar.

One of the Stabilisation Force's tasks was to hunt down those accused of war crimes. It would arrest several and hand them over to the International Criminal Tribunal in the Netherlands. The divisions were scaled down to brigade size in 2002 and then it was announced that the Stabilisation Force would be replaced by the European Union Force (EUFOR) at a NATO summit in December 2004. The force was reduced to just a few hundred men but it was still multinational. The task force may have been given a new name and the commanders may have changed but the objectives remained the same: Operation Althea would continue to enforce the peace across Bosnia and Herzegovina. The European Union Force took responsibility for all but one of the missions in the area, leaving the search for war criminals to the NATO headquarters based in Sarajevo.

The Kosovo War

The Socialist Republic of Serbia had cancelled the 1974 Yugoslav Constitution in September 1990. Oppression across Kosovo, where Orthodox Serbs and Kosovan Muslims lived side-by-side, then followed. All the Kosovar Albanians were sacked from the civil service and the Albanian media was shut down. The Kosovo Liberation Army was founded in 1996 to counter the tyranny; its members fought the Yugoslav Army throughout 1998, forcing one million people to leave their homes to escape the fighting. Religious and cultural buildings were destroyed and civilians were massacred, culminating in the murder of forty-five Kosovar Albanians in Račak in January 1999.

The Kosovans rejected NATO's wish to deploy a military peacekeeping force across the area while the Serbs refused to accept the peace agreement put in place, known as the Rambouillet Accords. So NATO had to resort to bombing the Serbs to the peace table, resulting in the signing of the Kumanovo Agreement in June 1999.

A NATO-headed peacekeeping force, called Kosovo Force (KFOR), deployed four multinational brigades across Kosovo to secure the area and disband the Kosovo Liberation Army. They removed ammunition dumps, held weapons amnesties and tackled arms smuggling, to reduce the number of armed confrontations. The peacekeepers protected Kosovan communities when possible or moved refugees from the war zones to safer areas; it then escorted humanitarian aid convoys to them.

KFOR then set up patrols and protected religious and cultural centres while the Interim Administration Mission took control of the area. Air and ground safety zones were implemented while mines and booby traps were removed from roads or mapped out for the peacekeepers. Security and civil forces were also deployed while all the heavy weapons were confiscated to make the area safe.

Over time, the Kosovo Force scaled down the security operations as it handed over responsibility for keeping the peace to the Kosovo Police. The war had resulted in over 13,500 deaths, many of them during the NATO airstrikes, while over 1.6 million people had been forced from their homes. The Kosovo Security Force was established in 2009 to take over all security tasks but a 4,000-strong multinational task force remains on standby in case any religious or ethnic violence flares up.

Insurgency in Macedonia

The Albanian National Liberation Army had been formed in 1999 to support the Albanian minority living in Macedonia, in southern Serbia; it would eventually number around 5,000 members. They didn't start fighting the Macedonian military until January 2001. The conflict peaked in the spring with the NLA controlling large parts of Macedonia. The Liberation

Army of Preševo, Medveđa and Bujanovac also engaged the Serbs across the Preševo valley. The fighting came to an end after the signing of the Ohrid Agreement in August 2001.

War Crimes

The Balkans war had demonstrated that the worst aspects of human nature could still emerge in Europe. There had been a blatant disregard for the 1949 Geneva Conventions, which laid down the rules for the humane treatment of wounded soldiers, prisoners of war and civilians. Injured soldiers had been murdered while their captured comrades had been forced to work under fire on military projects.

Soldiers and paramilitaries had removed or killed anyone ethnically different from them. Many people were intimidated into leaving their homes, often after members of their community had been murdered, to make way for other ethnic groups. Many were held in detention camps, where they endured terrible conditions. Churches were demolished, cemeteries were desecrated and cultural buildings were taken over; all part of the politicians' plans to claim an area.

Another disturbing aspect of the Balkans conflict was the use of rape. During the Bosnian War, Serb soldiers were encouraged to rape Bosniak women and girls, often in gangs, to impregnate them. They were then held in inhumane conditions in prison camps until their children were born. Around 35,000 Bosniak women and children were held in these so called 'rape camps' and many did not survive. Serbs did the same again against the Kosovo Albanians during the Kosovo War.

Many civilians were killed or injured during the indiscriminate shelling and bombing of their towns and villages. Around 14,000 were killed during the four-year-long siege of Sarajevo; another 13,500 people, many of them civilians, lost their lives during the Kosovo conflict.

The United Nations General Assembly went so far as to call the mass murder of Bosniaks by Serbs and Montenegrins across Bosnia and Herzegovina a genocide in resolution 47/121, issued in December 1992. It did not stop the worst incident of the conflict taking place at Srebrenica in July 1995: the massacre of 8,000 Muslim men and the sexual assault of hundreds of women.

Eventually, the International Court of Justice ruled in February 2007 that the Serbians had failed to stop the Republika Srpska carrying out the massacres and forced relocations. The court would eventually convict the

Bosnian Serb leader Radovan Karadžić of genocide, war crimes and crimes against humanity.

The Consequences

Violence had started with minor border clashes across Slovenia and Croatia in 1991 but it rapidly escalated into a deadly confrontation which affected tens of thousands of people. Serb and Croat forces would engage in an all-out war which resulted in 20,000 deaths and 250,000 refugees. It was then Bosnia and Herzegovina's turn between 1992 and 1995, as the Serbs set about driving the Bosniaks out. Nearly 100,000 were killed, another 250,000 were injured, while the number of refugees and displaced people rose to over 2.5 million. The war in Kosovo between 1998 and 1999 resulted in another 10,000 killed and another 850,000 people having to leave the region; several hundred thousand more were temporarily forced to leave their homes.

Over the course of ten years of fighting, over 130,000 people lost their lives, most of them civilians. Around 2.4 million left their country to escape the violence while another 2 million were forced to leave their homes; 1.5 million would never return.

The conflict had also caused enormous collateral damage, with over half the region's buildings suffering damage from shellfire and bombing. Great swathes of countryside were covered in landmines; Bosnia alone was estimated to be strewn with five million of the deadly weapons. It meant the legacy of the war continued as areas were cleared or marked off; around 1,500 people would be killed and many more maimed by landmines.

The estimated repair and replacement bill was estimated at $60 billion. Sanctions against the Federal Republic of Yugoslavia and hyperinflation of the Yugoslav dinar of 300 million per cent ruined the area's economy and around one million people lost their jobs, resulting in untold hardships for their families for many years.

The International Criminal Tribunal

The United Nations established the International Criminal Tribunal in 1993 with instructions to prosecute war criminals connected with the conflicts in Yugoslavia. It would sit in The Hague until the Mechanism for International Criminal Tribunals took over its duties in 2010. It finalised the cases against the war criminals until it closed in 2017.

Serbs, Croats and Bosniaks alike were accused of many crimes associated with ethnic cleansing, including intimidation, inhumane treatment, forced relocation and murder. Politicians were accused of encouraging and facilitating these policies, generals were accused of carrying them out. Some cases dragged on for years as the accused appealed against their long sentences. Many of the main participants in Europe's deadliest conflict since the Second World War are still serving long custodial sentences.

Index